From Me to We:
The Five Transformational Commitments
Required to Rescue the Planet,
Your Organization, and Your Life

There's a lot of unease and anger around at the moment at the state of our economies. "The System" is clearly not working, and the debate about alternatives to today's model of unsustainable capitalism is an increasingly lively one. But *From Me To We* invites us to dig a little deeper into why it is that the system isn't working, to interrogate the faulty philosophical "software" on which that system operates. Only then can we develop appropriate "rules" to guide the behavior of both individuals and organizations in taking forward those alternatives. This is a thoughtful, timely, and hugely significant contribution to today's all-important politics of transformation.
Jonathon Porritt, Chancellor of Keele University, UK; Founder, Director and Trustee, Forum for the Future UK; author, *Capitalism as if the World Matters*

Every business today needs a simple framework to guide their efforts to enhance their social, economic, and environmental performance. The five transformative commitments described by Bob Doppelt in his engaging new book provide a much-needed and compelling set of first-order principles that can guide every organization toward true sustainability.
Hunter Lovins, president, Natural Capitalism Solutions; author of *Climate Capitalism: Capitalism in the Age of Climate Change*, *Natural Capitalism: Creating the Next Industrial Revolution* and *The Natural Advantage of Nations*

I have given hundreds of Gore-inspired climate change slide shows, and I am always struck how each individual wonders how their individual actions can affect such a large, global problem. Doppelt's book effectively connects individual change and action to the global solution. Indeed, individual action and change must happen *before* the climate crisis can be solved globally.
Bill Bradbury, Former Oregon Secretary of State; Commissioner, Northwest Power and Conservation Planning Council

High time we broke free from the I-dolatry of the high consumer era, and started thinking about the community. This book points a way down that path.
Bill McKibben, author of *Eaarth: Making a Life on a Tough New Planet*

Bob has become the Stephen Covey of the sustainability movement. He has a knack for simplifying complexities. I use his three-step "borrow–use–return" business model as the epitome of a sustainable enterprise. I use his seven organizational blunders as a foil to sustainable governance. In this book he goes deeper. His five commitments reframe prerequisite personal and organizational mind-sets for a sustainable environment, society, and economy. Without them, sustainable business models and governance don't work. An inside-out approach to change is profound. Bob quick-starts our journey by shortlisting the proven, essential five commitments. As he concludes, the action stage is up to us.
Bob Willard, author of *The Sustainability Advantage*

In Bob Doppelt's new book he eloquently charges us to take the moral responsibility to join together, to use the power of "we," to address the climate crisis we face. And he tells us how to get there, and how to do it right now.
Kitty Piercy, Mayor, City of Eugene; Former Minority Leader of the House of Representatives

~

In *From Me To We*, Bob Doppelt identifies five commitments needed to transform the human race into a truly global society capable of avoiding the social and environmental catastrophes speeding our way. Given that some world's most threatening problems such as climate change will not be solved unless governments and individuals act in accordance with their global ethical responsibilities, this book makes an important contribution to our most civilization-challenging problems.
Donald A. Brown, Associate Professor of Environmental Ethics, Science, and Law, Penn State University; Program Director of the Collaborative Program on the Ethical Dimensions of Climate Change; author, *American Heat: Ethical Problems with the U.S. Response to Global Warming*.

~

Bob Doppelt's thorough and accessible *From Me to We: The Five Transformational Commitments Required to Rescue the Planet, Your Organization, and Your Life* explains how the urgent crises of climate and sustainability can only be resolved by changing how we think about ourselves and the world around us. To prevent our current trajectory leading to chaotic climatic turbulence and profound societal breakdown and hardship, we have the next decade in which to shift from an individualist (Me) to an interdependent (We) way of thinking and acting. Doppelt argues that this shift is possible, describes the five commitments we need to make, and shows how the shift from Me to We is not only critical for a sustainable way of life, but also good for our brain functioning and well-being. He also explains why many of us tend to struggle to make changes for greater sustainability. This book is a valuable resource for individuals, communities and organizations serious about preserving and sustaining life on our Earth.
Luisa M. Saffiotti, PhD, President, Psychologists for Social Responsibility, U.S.A.

~

Bob Doppelt brings welcome clarity and insight to the sustainable development debate. He reminds us that, if we want to change society, morals and culture matter. In a refreshing narrative, *From Me to We* shines the light of history, science, and spirituality on the challenge of systems change. With Doppelt's five commitments we now have a compass with which to navigate towards a more sustainable future.
Dr Wayne Visser, author of *The World Guide to CSR* and *The Age of Responsibility*; CEO, CSR International and Kaleidoscope Futures; Senior Associate, Cambridge University (Cambridge); Prof in Sustainability, Magna Carta College (Oxford)

Bob Doppelt is Executive Director of The Resource Innovation Group, a sustainability and climate change education, research, and technical assistance organization affiliated with the Center for Sustainable Communities at Willamette University, where he is also a Senior Fellow (www.theresourceinnovationgroup.org). He is also an adjunct instructor in the Department of Planning, Public Policy and Management at the University of Oregon. From 2002–2010 he directed Resource Innovations and the Climate Leadership Initiative in the Institute for a Sustainable Environment at the University of Oregon. His training and expertise is in counseling psychology and ecosystem science. Bob is the author of *The Power of Sustainable Thinking: How To Create a Positive Future for the Climate, The Planet, Your Organization, and Your Life* (Earthscan Publishing, 2008), which in 2011 was ranked as one of the 10 best books on climate change by *Audubon Magazine*. He is also the author of *Leading Change toward Sustainability: A Change Management Guide for Business, Government and Civil Society* (Greenleaf Publishing, 2003, 2011), which just six months after publication was ranked as one of the ten best publications on sustainability by a GlobeScan survey of international sustainability experts.

FROM ME TO WE

The Five Transformational Commitments Required to Rescue the Planet, Your Organization, and Your Life

BOB DOPPELT

LONDON AND NEW YORK

First published 2012 by Greenleaf Publishing Limited

Published 2017 by Routledge
2 Park Square, Milton Park, Abingdon, Oxon OX14 4RN
711 Third Avenue, New York, NY 10017, USA

Routledge is an imprint of the Taylor & Francis Group, an informa business

Copyright © 2012 Taylor & Francis

Cover by LaliAbril.com

All rights reserved. No part of this book may be reprinted or reproduced or utilised in any form or by any electronic, mechanical, or other means, now known or hereafter invented, including photocopying and recording, or in any information storage or retrieval system, without permission in writing from the publishers.

Notice:
Product or corporate names may be trademarks or registered trademarks, and are used only for identification and explanation without intent to infringe.

British Library Cataloguing in Publication Data:
 A catalogue record for this book is available from the British Library.

ISBN-13: 978-1-906093-71-6 (pbk)

To all of the *bodhisattvas* of the world who are
striving to wake up, do good work, and help
humanity prevent irreversible harm.

Contents

Acknowledgments viii

Introduction 1

   1 'Me' to 'We' throughout history 9

   2 The first commitment: See the systems you are part of 24

   3 The second commitment: Be accountable for all the consequences of your actions 40

   4 The third commitment: Abide by society's most deeply held universal principles of morality and justice 58

   5 The fourth commitment: Acknowledge your trustee obligations and take responsibility for the continuation of all life 92

   6 The fifth commitment: Choose your own destiny 115

   7 Conclusion: It is up to you 146

Endnotes 151

Index 160

Acknowledgments

No book is possible without the help of many past and current teachers, friends, and supporters. I give special thanks to the Buddha and the many other spiritual leaders who throughout time have clarified the true nature of the way the world works. I also want to thank my many professional colleagues in the field of psychology for their research and insights that have provided fact-based evidence of so much of what the world's spiritual leaders have long known. Thanks also to John Stuart, Dean Bargh, Rose Riddell, and the other staff at Greenleaf Publishing for their editorial assistance and overall support for this project. Finally, I offer deep gratitude to my soulmate, playmate, and one of the best and most honest editors in the world, my wife Peg.

Introduction

Economic breakdown, rising unemployment, and escalating political hostility, coming at a time of intensifying climate upheaval – storms, floods, heat waves, and droughts – have left us all confused and despondent. Everywhere we look, the systems we depend on seem to be collapsing.

Our first reaction is to blame others for these problems, be they greedy Wall Street bankers, rapacious corporations, or dishonest politicians of either the conservative or liberal persuasion.

But here's some news for you. Playing the blame game is merely an ingenious avoidance technique. It allows us to place the focus outside of ourselves and steer clear of having to look at our own contribution to today's troubling situations. Don't get me wrong. I know some people and organizations do bad things. But we often project onto others the very things we need to examine in ourselves.

The economic, social, and environmental ills we face today are of our own making. They are the outcomes of how we see and respond to the world. Unethical corporations and disreputable politicians might seem to cause the most egregious harm, but they are merely taking today's dominant cultural perspectives to the extreme. The challenges our society faces today illuminate the changes each of us needs to make in ourselves.

Even as we blame others for today's turmoil, many of us sense that something within us is deeply amiss. Our long-held assumptions and beliefs don't seem to explain the tumultuous events occurring all around us. We intuitively know that unprecedented changes are unfolding across the planet. We yearn for a way to make sense of these frightening events. But we don't know where to start.

Some of us try to mask our feelings of confusion and fear through distractions such as electronic games and non-stop social networking. Others sedate themselves with alcohol and drugs. Many seek to satisfy their deep thirst for meaning and purpose by consuming more and more material "stuff." These escapes briefly numb our feelings of despair; but never quench them.

To resolve a problem you first need to understand its cause. The roots of our troubles are simple, yet for most of us completely hidden from view. We have been living in a dream world, controlled by false perceptions and beliefs. Our personal lives, as well as the activities of the organizations with which we are involved, and society at large, have been guided by fundamental misjudgments about how our planet functions and what it means to live a good and decent life.

The most harmful illusion is that each of us exists on Earth as an independent, separate entity. This belief, now dominant in Western culture, in particular the U.S. and the UK, has produced an extreme form of individualism. Most of us today believe in the "sacredness" of the individual. Anything that threatens our ability to do whatever we want, whenever we want, is seen as a danger to our economy, personal freedom, and way of life.

The belief in separation leads us to accept the notion that self-interest is the dominant driver of human behavior. This is false. A selfless concern for the welfare of others is also encoded in our genes.[1] It is a powerful feedback that keeps the self-interested aspects of our personalities in check. By emphasizing only our selfish traits and denying our selfless qualities, we have denied our capacity for self-restraint and promoted behaviors that undermine the health of the planet and put billions of people in peril, including you and me.

Our belief in separation and the extreme individualism it has spawned is a fantasy – with startling consequences. It prevents us from seeing that we humans exist only due to the complex web of interlocking ecological and social systems that exist on Earth. Because we have failed to restrain our activities to conserve those systems, the Earth's surface temperatures are on a trajectory to rise by around 2°C, and possibly much more this century.[2] If this occurs, the consequences will be disastrous. Temperatures might climb gradually, in fits and starts, for a while. But then sudden shocking changes that no computer model could ever predict are likely to occur. Rapid and chaotic climatic shifts will trigger destructive heat waves or long-term drought, followed by food shortages, resources wars, and maybe the destruction of a major city or two by rising sea levels or horrific storms. Without a swift, dramatic change in direction, the coming decades will be a wild and turbulent ride.

To navigate the troubled waters that lie ahead and eventually emerge in a healthier condition, we must overcome the erroneous perspectives that have led to this predicament. At the most fundamental level, this involves a shift from responding to the world exclusively through the perspective of extreme individualism – the lens of "Me," which includes our personal, family, and organizational goals and desires – to meeting our needs by renewing and caring for an expansive "We" – the many people, organisms, and interconnections we are part of that make life possible and worthwhile.

Every human is born with the capacity to nurture the "We" that creates and supports us. But a number of factors today conspire to block this natural faculty. With focused effort, it *is* possible to overcome the obstructions and act in ways that sustain species, processes, and people beyond ourselves. If we break free of the falsehoods that control our minds, and see the world for what it actually is, we can marshal our forces and undergo the decade or so of challenging work required to rebuild our ecological and social systems. Ultimately, society will end up better off. If we fail to wake up and make the needed changes, humanity will face centuries of hardship.

The secret to resolving today's rapidly growing suite of crises is a profound change in the way we think about ourselves, and the world around us. The power of thought has been taught by almost every religion and philosophy since the beginning of time. The great spiritual teachers and thinkers have consistently told us that our lives are expressions of our inner assumptions, beliefs, and reasoning.

Three thousand years ago the Greek philosopher Hermes said, "As within, so without."[3]

The Bible says, "As a man thinketh in his heart, so is he."[4]

Hinduism teaches, "Your success or failure depends entirely on the quality of your thought."[5]

The Buddha declared, "All that we are is a result of what we have thought."[6]

More recently, Albert Einstein is said to have written, "The world we have created is a product of our thinking; it cannot be changed without changing our thinking."

These insights point out that we co-create our reality. The things around us are real, but what we see and what we believe about them is, at all times, our own creation. Our perceptions and actions are always a reflection of our inner thoughts. This means that if we change our thinking, we can change our reality or, perhaps more accurately, actually see the world for what it is.

Throughout history, humanity has altered its core assumptions and beliefs a number of times. In our earliest days, for instance, we thought human sacrifice was necessary for the survival of our clan. Our thinking shifted and the practice disappeared.

In ancient Athens women were classified as minors, always ruled by their father, brother, or some other male kin. After persistent challenges to this thinking, equality for women is now considered a fundamental right in most Western nations, and it is growing around the world as well.

According to the dominant cultural narrative of 500 years ago, the Earth was the center of the universe. Copernicus and Galileo challenged this belief, and, despite the initial resistance to this new perspective, humanity adapted its thinking to the reality that the Earth orbits around the Sun.

Just 150 years ago slavery was considered a normal and necessary institution by many religions and governments. It took remarkable courage and diligence to overcome the ferocious defense of the practice by slave owners and their supporters. Slavery in most nations is now seen as a basic violation of human rights and has been outlawed.

In the early 1970s chlorofluorocarbons (CFCs) used in aerosol spray cans and refrigerants were found to be depleting the Earth's ozone layer. CFC industry executives hotly disputed this, with one calling the science a "fiction tale ... a load of rubbish ... and utter nonsense."[7] Despite this opposition, by 1987 the Montreal Protocol, which phases out ozone-depleting substances, was established. By 2009 all countries in the United Nations (UN) had signed up.[8]

These are but a few examples of the new perspectives humans have adopted throughout time. With each change in thinking, most people, and society as a whole, ended up in substantially better shape. This shows that if we open ourselves to seeing the world in new ways, profound adjustments in our assumptions and beliefs about ourselves, other people, and the natural environment can come about.

As opposed to "first-order change" which slightly improves the efficiency of a system without fundamentally changing its goals, structures, or ultimate outcomes, the shift from "Me" to "We" constitutes a "second-order change," which establishes altogether new and truly sustainable objectives, designs, and results.[9] As we make this transformational shift, our personal awareness will increase and the fear and emptiness that pervade us will diminish. We can once again find promise, meaning, and inspiration in our lives.

And so we have come to an historic moment of choice. Do we continue our course of ever-increasing harm to nature, other people, and ourselves, driven by the illusion that we exist independently from other people and processes on Earth? Or do we abandon this destructive path and accept that our health and happiness is inherently linked to the well-being of others and to the planet's climate and ecological systems? Either option will be difficult. One thing is certain, however: continuing with business-as-usual will lead to catastrophe.

A growing army of people has chosen the latter path – the path that expands their thinking and behavior from an exclusive focus on themselves, to achieving their goals by nurturing and cooperating with the other people, organisms, and interconnections that exist on the planet. This massive grassroots movement includes over a million non-governmental, religious, and community organizations working for a fundamental shift in thinking.[10] It also includes multitudes of individuals striving to live their lives at peace with the natural environment and their fellow humans. If you change your thinking, you too can become part of this movement.

The emerging, though still fragile, new way of seeing and responding to the world – the "second-order" shift from "Me" to "We" that is the foundation of what I call sustainable thinking and action – suggests that a breakthrough moment is near. But it is by no means assured. Systems always push back hardest when threatened by meaningful change. Those who benefit the most from the "Me Only" way of thinking and acting are threatened by the upsurge and are working overtime to snuff it out and retain control.

This resistance can be overcome, however, if you, and the many others like you, find the courage to shed the erroneous beliefs that control your life. If you reclaim your power to see the world clearly and without prejudice, then a shift from "Me" to "We" will be possible. This transition will give us the wisdom and strength to persevere through the ten-year or so span of demanding effort that will be needed to shift gears and adopt sustainable ways of living.

Five powerful commitments described in the following chapters can help you make the conversion from focusing exclusively on "Me" to consistently accounting for the many people, organisms, and interdependencies involved with an emphasis on "We." None of the commitments is actually new. On the contrary, throughout human history sages have proclaimed them to be universal truths. They are often discussed today in a disjointed way, and at times you might practice one or more of them.

Although not particularly complicated, these five commitments are profoundly important because they are based on "natural laws" of sustainability. These are universal truths about how humans must interact with the Earth's ecological systems and with each other if we are to successfully transition through the rocky times ahead and emerge in a better condition.

The value of making the five commitments explicit is that it turns how you think and act into a cohesive and conscious choice. The ability to choose what we think about is the most powerful tool we have for controlling our lives and the future of our organizations. We expand our choices by altering our interpretations of the world. As I will discuss later in the book, the intentional act of focusing your attention on specific forms of thinking and behaviors can actually alter the way your mind functions and produce remarkable change.

This is important because our failure to live sustainably is not, at its core, the outcome of malevolent markets, inefficient technologies, or bad policy. Rather, it is a human problem, caused by the greatest crisis of human thought and imagination in history. Our ability to plot a safe course through the tumultuous times ahead will be determined by our willingness to alter our assumptions and beliefs about how the planet functions and to reassess how we must live and relate to each other. After more than 25 years of work in the field it has become clear to me that at this moment in time, the five natural laws and associated commitments described in the following pages provide the fundamentals needed to guide this transformation. They form the basis of all true 21st-century sustainability.

Each of the commitments can be applied immediately. You don't need to wait for other people or institutions to change. You and your organization only need to change your own thinking and behavior.

Each time you put the commitments into practice, the myths that have such a powerful hold on you will be weakened. You and the groups you engage with will then be better equipped to do your part to resolve the systemic breakdowns that threaten us all.

As you make the shift from "Me" to "We" that is at the heart of sustainable thinking and action, an extraordinary inner journey will begin that will radically change your life. Your optimism about the future and your self-confidence will grow. Hope and inspiration will be your hallmarks. You will become a beacon of light for others to follow.

1
'Me' to 'We' throughout history

In his late twenties Steve Aherns felt compelled to start his own home remodeling and construction business.[11] He grew up in a working-class neighborhood of Chicago, the only boy in a family of five with devoutly religious parents. Numerous aunts, uncles, and cousins continuously circled through the Aherns' residence. The deeply enmeshed family relations and strong religious overlay of Steve's upbringing left him feeling trapped in a suffocating net of expectations and demands. Launching his business was a way to break free of the constraints, strike out on his own, and achieve independence.

Steve's workaholic tendencies and constant striving to stay ahead of his competitors made his business a success. By his mid thirties he had 15 employees and two or three major construction projects under way most of the time. He often worked late into the night, went home to sleep for a few hours, and then returned to the office in the morning, long before anyone else arrived.

A few years after he started the business Steve married Irene. The early years of their marriage were good. The first of their two children was born 18 months after they tied the knot. Soon, however, his frequent absences, and preoccupation with work even when he was at home, left Irene and the children feeling neglected and abandoned.

Steve was not only a disengaged husband and father at home, he was also a demanding boss. Any employee who regularly disagreed with him was dismissed. He was unable to maintain long-term friendships.

Government regulations were a constant thorn in Steve's side. It was easier and more profitable to build homes on undeveloped greenfield sites, and he put constant pressure on local authorities to open up forest and farmland for housing projects. Speed was essential in his business because the quicker one job was completed the sooner another could begin. To save time and money he did the absolute minimum to comply with health and safety, labor, and environmental regulations.

After ten years of success a series of crises occurred that changed his life forever. To cut costs, Steve installed cheap drywall in a number of his construction projects. He also used the drywall in the bedroom additions he built for his daughters at his personal residence. After a while, the people who purchased the houses Steve built began to complain about sneezing, nasal congestion, skin rashes, and itching. Steve immediately dismissed their claims, saying it had nothing to do with him. But then one of his daughters was suddenly stricken by extreme shortness of breath and heavy wheezing. It was a severe attack of asthma. In a fit of panic, Irene rushed her to the hospital where she was stabilized.

It turned out the cheap drywall was filled with toxic substances and had become moldy. The black mold gave off corrosive gases that were extremely toxic.

The owners of the toxic homes sued Steve and his company, causing his insurance company to pay out a huge settlement. The bad publicity that followed led to the demise of his business.

Irene was furious with Steve for putting their children at risk. She decided enough was enough, took the children, moved out, and filed for divorce.

These shocking events caused Steve to take a step back and evaluate his life. He came to realize that his absolute insistence on freedom from personal constraints, and his "what's in it for me?" thinking and behavior had cost him his business, denied him meaningful friendships, and tarnished his reputation in the community. Most importantly, it had put his children at risk and destroyed his family life. Steve's way of viewing and responding to the world left him empty and isolated, with a deep loss of self-esteem.

After much soul-searching, Steve made a fundamental decision. He still wanted autonomy from the tight controls of his childhood, but he now had a deeper understanding that his life had little meaning unless he shared it with others. He decided to commit his life to helping people. He would give much greater attention to the natural environment. He vowed to rebuild his relationship with his children. He also hoped to find someone now to share his life with, and he was determined to give that person the care and attention he had denied Irene. Through these changes he hoped to restore his personal dignity. Steve had made the transition from "Me" to "We."

Steve's story is the story of us all. Our self-focused "Me First and Only" thinking and behavior has produced tragic consequences for the natural environment, other people, our loved ones, and ourselves.

Just as Steve's dysfunctional behavior was in large part a reaction to his early experiences, the starting point for resolving today's rapidly growing suite of crises is to understand that our dominant ways of viewing and responding to the world are the vestiges of thinking that emerged three centuries ago in response to conditions that no longer exist. We must now dig deep and do what is necessary to update our perspectives to conform to today's realities. This requires a "second-order" shift from focusing only on our personal and family needs and wants, and those of our organizations – on "Me" – to getting what we need and desire by enhancing the well-being of other people, communities, and the planet's climate and ecological systems – by prioritizing "We."

'Me' to 'We' in human psychosocial development

Each period of our lives brings new challenges. As new complexities emerge, humans naturally shift their perspectives back and forth from a self-focused emphasis on "Me" to a more selfless concern for "We." Sometimes, however, people get stuck in one stage as they age and fail to move on to the next. That's when many emotional and psychological troubles begin. Psychologist Erik Erikson developed a theory of the stages of human psychosocial development that offers a useful framework for understanding this dynamic.[12]

The days and weeks immediately after birth are the first "Me" period. Your total focus is on obtaining the food, warmth, and safety you need to survive. Within a few months, however, you begin to realize that your parents, and your mother in particular, provide the sustenance and nurturing that allow you to survive. This marks your first vague awareness that your well-being depends on the care of others.

Somewhere around the age of two you begin to explore your surroundings and assert your independence. The "terrible twos," as it is commonly known, constitutes another egocentric "Me" period. This is your first attempt to distinguish between yourself and the outside world, and to assert your independence.

From 6 to 12 you develop an initial sense of self-confidence. You discover unique talents and special interests. You strive to be responsible, to be good, and to do things the right way. You also realize that your sense of self depends on how your parents and friends respond to you. You are therefore more willing to share and cooperate with others than you might have been earlier in your young life. This is another "We" stage of development when your needs are met by cooperating with the people around you.

Then comes adolescence. The years from 10 to 18 or so are definitely a strongly self-focused "Me" period. You are concerned about how you appear to others. You try different ways of relating to people in order to see what type of outer behavior best matches your inner sense of self. In the later stages of adolescence you develop a sexual identity. Through many trials and tribulations you develop an initial sense of who you are and where your life is headed.

Your twenties are likely to be a time of transition from focusing almost exclusively on "Me" to also emphasizing "We." You are eager to be accepted by others while making your own way in the world. You therefore try to mesh your personal identity with that of your friends while striving to maintain your independence.

For most people growing up in Western societies, the struggle between self-focused thinking and behavior and sacrificing some of what we want in order to gain meaningful engagement with others – an important aspect of shifting from "Me" to "We" – often continues until about the age of 30. Somewhere around that age the tension begins to come to an end, though for some people it can continue at the margins for the rest of their lives.

After establishing a personal identity, adults become able to form intimate relationships with other people through close friendships and marriage. When your sense of self is sufficiently robust, you are much more willing to make the compromises and sacrifices required to maintain such relationships. In contrast, adults who lack sufficient self-identity often fail to form intimate relationships throughout their entire lives.

During the middle ages of life, from 40 to 60 years, most people with a solid sense of self adopt a "We" perspective that includes guiding future generations or contributing to society. Raising a family or involvement with the community offers a deep sense of personal accomplishment and satisfaction. Your needs are met by focusing on a larger "We." This is true maturity.

An adult who has failed to develop a sufficient sense of self, on the other hand, might remain self-focused and unwilling to help other people or the community at large. Their continual "Me" orientation leaves them angry and dissatisfied with life.

Erikson's framework helps us understand that it is natural for human beings to shift their focus back and forth between "Me" and "We" as they confront the new challenges that emerge in different periods of their lives. As we grow, sometimes the self-focused aspects of our personality dominate, and at other times the cooperative and selfless parts of us reign supreme. We are naturally endowed with both qualities. People are the happiest and most fulfilled, however, when their needs are met by caring for others. That is, when they focus on "We."

'Me' to 'We' in human cultural development

The evolution of human cultures can be viewed through a similar lens. Throughout history, in response to problems that were often created by the previous culture, societies have shifted back and forth from a dominant focus on "Me" to different variations of an emphasis on "We." Societies that failed to alter their cultural beliefs and practices when conditions changed experienced long periods of social strife and impoverishment, and many perished.[13] Societies that successfully responded to new conditions by adopting new perspectives survived and thrived.

Early humans were predominantly hunters and gatherers. Much like a newborn baby, they were almost exclusively focused on satisfying their physiological needs. People lived for the present moment, with little concern for the well-being of others. It was very much a survivalist "Me" period of human history.

Over time, however, humans evolved from hunters and foragers to agriculturalists. People came to realize there was safety in numbers and they could grow more food by working together. The first "We" period of human cultural development emerged when, in various times and places, humans organized themselves into clans and tribes.

Because clans and tribes derived their subsistence directly from the land, most saw themselves as intimately tied to nature. Animistic and mystical beliefs dominated. They believed that souls or spirits existed in humans as well as in rocks, plants, mountains, and even natural phenomena such as lightening and floods. If the crops failed during a full moon, for example, people concluded that one event caused the other.[14]

To live together as peacefully as possible, clans developed social rules. Each member of the clan had to submit to the rules or take the risk of being ostracized, cast out from the tribe, or worse. People sacrificed their personal identities to remain part of the group.

However, clans and tribes often became vulnerable to charismatic leaders who used a fear of evil spirits and mysticism to keep people in line. Unhappiness emerged when the chieftain's superstitious pronouncements about "truth" proved to be false, which undermined their authority. The regimented thinking and behavior required to live in the clan also began to rub people up the wrong way.

Emulating the adolescent's natural desire to separate from their parents and develop their own identity, the clannish "We" period of human cultural development broke down and humanity entered another powerful "Me" phase, this time dominated by a focus on individual autonomy, strength, and power.

Although historians disagree on the exact dates to assign this period, there is a general consensus that it spanned from about 300 to 800 A.D. With no mystical spirits or cultural rules to control them, during the Early Medieval Period, or so-called "Dark Ages," people exerted the dominating aspects of their personalities with little regard for the consequences. It was a time of chaos and go-it-alone hedonism. The weak were exploited by the strong without guilt. People once again lived only for the here and now.[15]

During this period, subsistence agriculture, hunting, and fishing remained the primary sources of food, energy, and raw materials. Nature thus continued to be seen as intimately connected to human activities.[16]

This era of human cultural development came to an end when people grew tired of living in constant chaos and fear. The random destruction of this potent "Me" period also left people isolated and alone, with no one to care for or about them.

And so began the next "We" stage of human cultural evolution in Europe called the "Middle Ages." This was a time of feudalism when humans once again sacrificed their independence and formed allegiances to higher authorities in order to obtain a sense of order and safety.

In the feudal state, kings or their lords controlled the land and gave permission to peasants to use it in exchange for some type of service, such as military activity.[17] Powerful religious institutions, dominated by the Church, supported the feudal state. The Church controlled the hearts and minds of people by promoting the idea that a force much greater than themselves determined their lives. Material gains were to be forgone in order to obtain future rewards in the hereafter.

Despite the focus on the next life, even in the Middle Ages nature was seen as a dynamic mother-like entity that could sometimes be nurturing and kind but at other times vicious and unforgiving.[18]

Over time, however, the bureaucracies that grew to administer the feudal state became demanding and authoritarian. Religious leaders became increasingly doctrinaire by proclaiming that only they knew God and that their way was the "only true way." Unless you were lucky enough to be born into the top echelons of society, you lived a life of poverty.

The lack of personal freedom created a sense of bitterness that led to a desire for self-determination. The poor got fed up with their lot and began to demand increased material well-being in the here and now. People also saw that more than one "truth" existed in the world.

Thus began the next "Me" era of human cultural development that scholars call the "Enlightenment" or the "Age of Reason." Beginning in Europe between 1650 and 1700, and lasting until about 1800, this cultural movement reacted to the intolerance and controls of feudal lords and the Church by emphasizing each individual's capacity to think for themselves. People began to use their own initiative and creativity to increase their immediate material well-being. The foundations of today's "Western" worldview began to emerge.

Evolution of the Western worldview

Although numerous people contributed to the development of the Western perspective, the French philosopher René Descartes (1596–1650) was among the most influential. He said that because God created the world, it was imbued with unalterable laws that operated with clockwise precision. These laws could be understood through the use of deductive reasoning and logic.

Rather than attributing events such as earthquakes and floods to evil spirits or angry gods, nature began to be seen as a machine composed of small separate parts. A new concept of the self as a rational planner, housed in a machine-like body that controlled human emotions was crystallized. This notion, which replaced the idea that people were intimately linked to the cosmos, provided a cognitive basis for a split between human consciousness and the rest of nature.[19]

Sir Isaac Newton (1642–1727) then spelled out in mathematical terms the mechanical principles of force and motion. This validated Descartes' idea of a mechanical universe.

To these ideas, John Locke (1632–1704), a British philosopher and political theorist, added the notion that God intended humans to own land and doing so was simply God's will. He also asserted that cultivating land for production was a sign of merit with the end being "riches and power" that were essential for national defense.[20]

Thomas Hobbes (1588–1679) soon proposed a view of human nature that eliminated the religious justification for land ownership. He said the basis of human nature is competitive self-interest. To establish some semblance of order in the competitive world people must enter into contracts when doing business. This required some type of government. But the state should leave the people alone to accumulate material wealth because what is good for the individual will eventually be good for the state.[21]

The Protestant reformers, led by Martin Luther and John Calvin, also made a major contribution to Western thinking by reinserting the religious justification for material acquisition that was lost in the Hobbesian view. The Calvinists declared work to be a divine calling and that material rewards were God's blessing for a job well done. The wealthy merely reflected God's approval, while the poor deserved what they got because of their lack of effort. This led to what is now known as the "Protestant ethic":

work and the wealth it creates are good; laziness and the poverty it leads to are a sin.[22]

These views became widely accepted when, in 1776, Adam Smith published *An Inquiry into the Nature and Causes of the Wealth of Nations*.[23] He proclaimed that if each individual pursued his or her own self-interest the "invisible hand" of the market would make society better off.

It is important to remember that Smith formulated his views during a time when almost all trade occurred within small communities, the world had a fifth as many people as it does today, except in small isolated cases few resources were depleted, and the Earth's climate was stable. Under those circumstances, Smith's theory provided further support for the belief that we each stand alone as an independent entity with little to no responsibility for anything beyond ourselves. Interdependency came to be seen as a weakness rather than a strength.

Just a few years later, in 1780, Eli Whitney introduced the idea of interchangeable parts, which revolutionized the manufacturing industry and triggered the start of the Industrial Revolution. Factories producing an increasing number of basic goods sprang up in the northern U.S., UK, and other parts of Europe.

The belief in "reductionism" surfaced as scientists discovered that breaking things down into little pieces and studying each of the parts in isolation could expand their capacity to understand and manipulate nature to increase material well-being. Working life became more specialized.

Even though industrialization made different geographic regions, industries, and sectors of the economy more interlinked than ever before, the form of organization used to manage the system made the interdependency increasingly difficult to see. Until that point in history people performed almost all of the tasks required to meet their basic needs for food, shelter, and warmth. In the industrial system, they could no longer directly see where their raw materials came from, how things were made, where their waste ended up, or what the consequences of these activities would be for other people, their environment, or themselves.

These and other changes reinforced the belief in separation and individualism. The individual came to be viewed as the only reality. Personal autonomy and independence from others became the most cherished goals. All problems came to be seen almost exclusively as individual matters that were, at best, marginally influenced by the social, economic, or political arrangements of the past or present.

The self-focused 'Me' worldview of Western society today

Much of Western society today, especially the U.S. and UK, remains largely organized around these beliefs. Extreme individualism reigns supreme. Just as the "Me" stages of human psychosocial development emphasize the self-focused aspects of our personalities and downplay the selfless elements, our present "Me" stage of cultural development accentuates individual self-interest and discounts the innate caring and cooperative aspects of our nature.

Although variations exist, and people might feel more passionately about some of the elements than others, in general today's Western worldview consists of five primary ideas:[24]

- Each human is a separate being that exists independently from all other humans and from the planet's climate and ecological systems.

- Because each of us is a separate, independent being we are responsible only for ourselves. Anything that constricts our ability to do what we want, when we want, as long as we do not materially harm other people, is bad.

- Humans are instinctively driven to achieve private, mostly economic gain, and the market is the natural neutral arbiter of competition for these resources.

- Nature is composed of separate, mostly inert elements that humans have the right to manipulate and control for material gain.

- Continuous "progress" driven by ongoing economic growth is essential and possible because human ingenuity will always find ways to overcome scarcity and constraints.

This worldview has produced many positive outcomes. It has channeled the tremendous energy of our current adolescent period of human cultural development into scientific and technological innovations that have relieved many of the physical burdens and risks associated with feeding and housing ourselves. Achievements in medicine have solved the mysteries of many age-old illnesses and diseases, and extended the human lifespan. Hard-working people have seen their ingenuity and output linked to economic rewards. Most people in our forward-looking society enjoy unparalleled material well-being, especially when compared to 100 years ago and to poor regions of the world today.[25]

Like the worldviews held by all previous cultures throughout history, however, the Western belief in separation and extreme individualism has produced its own set of unique problems. The unsustainable nature of the world's economic system – based on constantly growing material and energy consumption powered by the use of fossil fuels, unregulated trade, and financial speculation – is now readily apparent. Economic and political power has become concentrated in the hands of a small group of wealthy corporate and financial interests. Disparities between rich and poor have become extreme. A large percentage of the populace feels a deep sense of alienation, loneliness, and lack of meaning in their lives. Most importantly, we have overshot the limits of our ecological systems and produced climate disruption and ecosystem degradation that now threatens the very basis of human civilization.

These and other problems make clear that, just as Steve Aherns needed to fundamentally reorient his thinking and behavior in order to reconstruct his life, if we are to successfully respond to the difficult years that lie ahead and transition to true sustainability, Western society must make a "second-order" shift from its current "Me" stage of cultural development to the next "We" phase. We must meet our physical, emotional, and psychological needs by cooperating with, and caring for, people across the planet, and by restoring the natural environment. To make this change we must constrain our self-focused instincts and amplify our innate selfless qualities.

This is not a utopian dream. As we have just seen, in response to problems that were created by the previous worldview, throughout history societies have continually shifted their thinking and practices back and forth between a dominant focus on "Me" to different varieties of an emphasis on "We." None of the transitions was easy. Each involved intense conflict between people devoted to the existing worldview and those committed to a new perspective. Each conversion was made even more complicated by the fact that every human starts life in a "Me" stage. When the dominant cultural narrative of their day emphasized "Me," they had to overcome great impediments to reach a mature and healthy "We" stage of personal psychosocial development. But even with these obstacles, numerous large-scale shifts in cultural perspectives have occurred throughout time.

Our current self-focused "Me" stage of cultural development has produced numerous crises because it violates the natural laws that govern the way people must relate to each other and the planet today if civilization is to remain viable and prosper. It is imperative that you, and many others like you, bring your thinking and behavior into line with contemporary conditions so that society can rapidly transition to the next "We" stage of cultural development.

In making this shift, the intrinsic altruistic and caring aspects of your character will be maximized, which will increase your sense of integrity and well-being. You can then help other people, and the organizations you participate in, make a similar transition.

The five natural laws and associated commitments that follow will help you and your organization plot a safe course through this tumultuous period of human history to come out the other side in a more secure and sustainable condition.

2

The first commitment
See the systems you are part of

How do you see the world? Does your image include all of the things that actually exist on the planet, or is your vision narrowly focused on your personal, family, or organizational needs and wants?

Most of us are not so self-centered as to say that we completely ignore the natural environment or other people. Nor will most people or organizations say they are always selfless and think only of others. But if your focus is mostly limited to your personal or organizational desires, then time and again you will think about little else and fail to see how your activities affect other people, the natural environment, or even yourself.

The difference between an expansive view of the world and a restricted perspective can be understood by looking up from this book for a moment and taking several deep breaths. Feel the air as it fills your lungs. Can you explain what just happened?

Oxygen entered your body and sustained your life. Oxygen supports a process called cell respiration that turns food into energy. Oxygen also detoxifies your blood, strengthens your immune system, and rebuilds your body. Do you know how this oxygen came to be? About three-quarters of it was produced during photosynthesis in single-celled green algae and bacteria in marine environments. The remainder came from the same process in forests and other vegetation. Complex interactions occurring all around you created the oxygen that makes your life possible.

How conscious are you of these elaborate relationships? If you fail to consider the intricate web of interactions unfolding all around the planet, you will often act in ways that impair those life-giving forces. You will also create significant distress for other people – and, ultimately, for yourself.

We humans live in systems. You are a complex system yourself. Think of your heart, lungs, and the many other organs that work together seamlessly to keep your body running. You are also a member of numerous social systems, such as your family, place of work, community, professional societies, and fellow humans around the globe. Additionally, as the oxygen you just inhaled demonstrates, you are a part of the larger complex living system that is planet Earth.

The reality is that everything on the planet is created and sustained by something else. There is nothing that actually exists by itself. This is the **Law of Interdependence.** It is the most fundamental of all the natural laws of sustainability. It says that each of us exists in this world only as part of a complex web of interlocking systems. There is no truly separate "Me." Each person is created and sustained by interconnected networks of ecological and social systems – a collective "We."

Most of us intuitively know this. We recognize that the air we breathe, the food we eat, and the water we drink are produced by natural processes, and that our loved ones are important to our well-being. But too often we ignore this basic fact of life. Outdated assumptions and beliefs lead us to think and act as if we are independent entities that can exist without the interactions with, and influences of, other processes, organisms, or people.

Only when you broaden your awareness and see the threads that unite all of creation will you understand who you truly are as a human. Only when you consider the other parts of the systems you are part of will you see the truth about how the world functions. Only when you are conscious of the integrated nature of the systems that created and support you will you gain an accurate sense of what is needed to sustain life on the planet, including yourself and your organization.

Understanding the context in which you exist is essential for progress toward true sustainability. **The first, and most important commitment you and the organizations you are involved with must make to realize the shift from "Me" to "We" that is essential to resolving today's many crises, is to see the systems you are part of.**

After scores of people and organizations make this commitment, society will take the first step toward maneuvering through the tumultuous days that lie ahead in a manner that eventually resolves our interlocking social, economic, and ecological problems. Not coincidently, the more aware you become of the many ways in which your life is completely dependent on the larger whole, the greater your personal happiness and well-being.

This commitment is extremely important because it focuses your attention on **integration**. All of the other commitments involved with the shift from "Me" to "We" follow from this foundational principle.

Healthy ecological, social, and economic systems are integrated. Individual elements function as complete wholes while, at the same time, functioning harmoniously as interdependent aspects of many other elements and processes. The integrated nature of a system allows it to adapt to changing circumstances without losing its essential properties.

Dysfunctional systems, on the other hand, lack integration. One or more elements or processes have become dominant or been seriously weakened. The system is no longer able to self-regulate. It has lost its resilience: the capacity to withstand and bounce back from insults without changing its core structure and functions. Extreme rigidity, or the opposite – chaos – might result as the system is pushed over a threshold into a new, undesirable (from a human perspective) condition.

The more you see the systems you are dependent upon, the greater your understanding will be of the importance of integration.

What do I mean by a system? A system is a set of independent but interrelated elements that interact in ways that make them a unified whole. The computer this book was written on is an electronic system composed of hundreds of components working together in a way that produces digital images on a screen. Forest ecosystems include living and non-living elements that interact with each other in ways that generate some of the oxygen on which we all depend, and much more. Organizations are collections of people who have been arranged in ways to produce certain outcomes.

The components of a system can include physical objects that are easily seen or touched such as the trees and rocks in a forest ecosystem, or the parents and siblings that are part of your family's social system. They also include less concrete factors such as the sunlight and nutrients flowing through a forest or the unspoken but deeply held beliefs and social expectations of people in an organization that drives its performance.

None of these components by themselves constitute a system. A rock is not a system in itself. But when a rock is eroded by rain, snow, and ice causing sediments to contribute to soil formation, it becomes part of an ecological system. A single person is not a social system. However, when two people interact they become a social system.

The point is that it is the linkages between collections of elements that turn them into a system. Upon deeper examination, what appear to be separate entities turn out to be interwoven aspects of each other. Systems have a "wholeness" to them, with ongoing interactions and feedbacks that allow them to maintain that integration.[26]

Systems are nested within larger systems. A tree is a whole system in itself, composed of roots, trunk, branches, and leaves as well as vessels that connect everything by carrying water and nutrients throughout. A tree is also embedded within larger local ecological systems. These systems depend on patterns of moisture, heat, and sunlight that are determined by even larger regional weather systems. These weather systems are shaped by the Earth's oceans and climate system, which are shaped by interactions between the Sun and the Earth.

Similarly, when you were a baby your parents and siblings likely constituted your immediate social system. You were completely dependent on them for physical and emotional nurturing. Your parents were supported by a much larger social system that perhaps included their parents, siblings, and close friends. That system was embedded within an even larger social system that probably included co-workers, community members, and others.

Nothing exists on its own. This is a fundamental fact on our planet. No actual boundaries exist that firmly separate one human, or one plant, animal, or natural process from another. An intricate, interdependent web of climatic, ecological, and social systems creates and sustains all life on Earth, including you.

We believe our skin, and the skin of other creatures separates one organism from another. But the skin is merely the interface between the outer and inner aspects of a living being. It is created by bodily processes, fed by nutrients from the outside, and influenced by its internal and external environments. Indeed, the skin functions more as a connector than a separator.[27]

The borders we humans draw around things to distinguish one component from another, or this event from that one, are not real.

They are merely illusions created by our minds to help us make sense of the world by breaking it into smaller pieces.

Our failure to understand this reality causes much distress. Just as in a war, every boundary we draw becomes a battle line. The more we separate "Me" from "nature" and "Me" from "other people" the more we see everything outside of ourselves as a threat to be feared, controlled, or conquered.[28] It is impossible under these conditions to care for the ecological systems that created and sustain us. Nor can we trust or cooperate with other people. Loneliness, alienation, and emotional distress are the natural outcomes.

Powerful cultural narratives, however, born from the notions we inherited from our ancestors who lived centuries ago in conditions far different than ours today, advance the view that each of us exists and functions as a separate entity. Our parents learned this and passed it on to us. Our schools require us to memorize the names of different things as if knowing the label a human has given something explains the processes and interactions that make it what it is. Policy-makers approach economic, social welfare, public health, and environmental problems as if they are distinct from each other and require different remedies. The media, economic theory, and our political discourse reinforce this belief of separation.

This view is undeniably false. The truth is that from the climatic and biosphere that interact to keep the Earth at just the right temperature to support life, to the male and female that mated and gave you life, we are all made from, composed of, sustained, and affected by interdependent webs of social and ecological systems of all sizes, shapes, and functions. Thinking otherwise is a complete misrepresentation of reality.

Let us briefly explore some of these systems, starting with the largest one of importance to us humans, and moving to the smallest.

The most essential system from a human perspective is the one involving the Sun and the Earth. All of the energy on our planet comes from the Sun. Life on Earth would not exist without it.

The Sun shapes the Earth's climate system. This is a complicated system with many elements that interact to keep the planet at just the right temperature to support life as we know it. The climate system includes the atmosphere, the ocean, ice and snow cover, land surfaces, and the chemical, biological, and physical interactions occurring among them. All of these processes are driven by radiation from the Sun.

The surface of the Earth absorbs some of the heat produced by the Sun and reflects the remainder back into the atmosphere. A mixture of gases that naturally surround the Earth, including carbon dioxide, methane, nitrous oxide, and others, capture a portion of the reflected heat before it escapes into space. For the past 12,000 or so years the amount of greenhouse gases in the atmosphere has remained relatively constant. Just as the insulation in your home keeps temperatures comfortable, the natural "blanketing" effect of these gases keeps the planet livable. What we consider human civilization developed only because of this long period of relatively stable climate conditions.

Due to human activities, today the concentration of atmospheric greenhouse gases is more than a third higher than existed prior to the Industrial Revolution. As a result, the Earth's climate system has been disrupted and surface temperatures are rising. We will discuss this problem in more depth in the next chapter.

The Earth's climate system shapes all of the planet's other systems, including the biosphere which is the next largest and most important system from a human perspective. The biosphere is the roughly eight-mile (13 km)-thick zone of land, sea, and air surrounding the planet that supports life. It is composed of numerous biotic communities which are interdependent systems of plants and animals – including humans – that live in particular habitats.

Sunlight, heat, and precipitation patterns determined by local and regional weather systems interact with local soil types to determine the quantity and abundance of vegetation in an area. The Sun also drives photosynthesis within the biosphere, which maintains the oxygen level of the atmosphere. Nearly all life on Earth – including you and me – depend on photosynthesis directly or indirectly as a source of food and energy.

The organisms that compose a biotic community are completely dependent upon each other. If the trees die out in a forest, the animals that live there either die or move elsewhere because their source of food disappears and their habitat becomes too unforgiving due to the loss of the moderating influence of the trees.

The plants and animals that compose a biotic community are also inseparably linked by the materials flowing through them and by the magnitude of the natural forces acting on them. Phosphate, for instance, is an essential inorganic chemical that plants cannot live without. Phosphate would be unavailable to vegetation if bacteria did not decompose dead plants and animals and release the phosphate held in their carcasses back to the environment for now uses. These types of circular exchanges of materials and energy among living organisms, including us humans, and their environment are endlessly repeated on Earth. We call them ecological systems, or ecosystems.

Ecosystems can be as encompassing as the entire biosphere, they can cover large areas such as prairies, lakes, or forests, or they can be as tiny as a "balanced" aquarium. Ecosystems support biotic communities and biotic communities play a central role in ecosystems.

The climate and biosphere continuously influence each other. The Earth's response to change is much like the human body's response. When we become overheated, perspiration reduces our body temperature. In the same way, the Earth regulates itself through the ongoing interactions between the climate and biosphere. Radiation from the Sun, for instance, increases surface temperatures. This force is countered by feedbacks such as white surfaces like snow and ice that reflect the solar heat away from the Earth. The Earth is a dynamic yet relatively stable system due to strong feedbacks. To quote the European Geological Union: "The Earth system behaves as a single, self-regulating system comprised of physical, chemical, biological, and human components."[29]

Our planet is thus composed of millions of species of plants and animals, including *Homo sapiens*, all constantly using and reusing the same molecules of water, land, and air produced and circulated by complex ecological systems that are shaped by, and that influence, the global climate system. It is an undeniable truth that human economies, communities, and households exist only because of these integrated, interlocking self-regulating systems.

The inherent unity between what we typically call "the natural environment" and "humans" is critically important. If you do not understand that you are part of this interdependent whole, you will be unable to grasp how your actions might harm that unity.

The same principles apply to social systems that, from a human perspective, are the next most important system. Our lives depend upon, and are shaped by, an intricate web of relationships that include the people close by us as well as those living halfway around the globe.

You can identify the people involved in a social system by considering its purpose or function. If your purpose is to raise your children, then your kids, spouse, and perhaps other immediate family members, comprise your immediate social system. Your family requires food, energy, and a roof over their heads to keep them warm and dry. Your family system is therefore enmeshed within numerous larger social systems that have as their purpose the provision of those goods and services.

Some of these social systems might be local. The vegetables you eat, for instance, might come to you through the efforts and interactions among farmers, equipment suppliers, truckers, retailers, and others operating close to your home. Today, however, a vast majority of the goods you purchase, from fruit, to medicines, to shoes, include substances or components that are sourced from around the globe. Many people, young and old, rich and poor, of all colors, religious faiths, and cultures in far off places are thus likely to be members of your social system.

We often call the systems that work together to produce goods and services "economic" systems. This term is a misnomer because it takes the human element out of social systems that have the specific purpose of producing goods and services. After all, it is people that invest capital, create technologies, trade with each other, operate equipment, harvest crops, distribute products, provide services, and use materials and energy. Economic systems are merely systems of social relations organized for the specific purpose of producing and delivering goods and services.

The term "economy" also gives a misleading impression when it suggests that economic systems are somehow separate from the Earth's natural systems. We have drawn a boundary around and classified labor, capital, raw materials, buyers and sellers as the elements of an "economy" in order to measure and control inputs and outputs. But, like all other attempts to separate and categorize, these are imaginary divisions. The so-called "economy" is nothing more than a subset of all of the natural elements and interactions occurring on Earth.

Sometimes you see yourself at the top in a social system, sometimes you think you are in the middle, and at other times you believe you are at the bottom. When you imagine yourself on top you might believe that you made it there on your own. You deserve all that you have because of your wisdom, strength of character, and perseverance. Other people are the recipients of your knowledge, expertise, and goodwill. You are the teacher and others are the students. You are the manager and others are the workers. You are the leader and others are followers.

When you hold this perspective, those in the middle and at the bottom frequently appear to be weaker than you. You see them as mere accessories needed to carry out certain functions, not people central to your accomplishments or the performance of the overall system. Because you believe that you are the reason for your success, others rarely measure up to your standards.

Most times, however, quite the opposite is true. Your success was possible only because of the many people who came before you and those who now provide the support and resources you rely on to achieve your goals. Your role in the system is no more or less important than that of all others. Because your thinking ignores this reality, however, you sometimes purposely, and oftentimes inadvertently, establish hierarchies that lead to great inequalities in income, wealth, and power. These inequalities, in turn, erode the health and well-being of other people – and, ultimately, of yourself.[30]

When you see yourself at the bottom of a social system looking up, things look quite different. You might regularly see the tops and the middles as power-hungry higher-ups who don't understand you, are insensitive to your needs, or take advantage of you. When things don't go as you think they should you feel justified in criticizing "them" for their incompetence, selfishness, or cruelty. You are suspicious of the motives and integrity of those above you, yet you fear appearing inferior to them. You envy the material goods and lifestyle of the tops and middles, and often consume beyond your means in order to keep up. What you fail to realize is that often you have given away your power to those on top and participated in the creation of the very system you despise.

When you are in the middle of a social system you often feel squeezed by both sides. You aspire to become one of the tops. Status competition and fear of social disapproval drive much of your behavior. You acquire more and more material goods in order to be accepted by them. At the same time, you might often look down upon those at the bottom who you see as potential threats to your position in life, or as weak, lazy, or incompetent. Both the tops and the bottoms make unreasonable demands on you.

We habitually get caught up in these dynamics because we fail to see ourselves in relation to the other people involved in our social systems. When we create divides between others and ourselves, we imagine that we are detached, independent entities. This leads us to ignore the powerful ways in which the social systems we are involved with shape how others see and respond to us, and how we view ourselves and react to others.

Why is it that we humans fail to understand that we exist only because we are intimately linked to everything else? One of the reasons is that survival for our hunter–gatherer ancestors required self-absorption. We had to continually protect ourselves from saber-toothed tigers and other threats. Self-focused tendencies became deeply embedded in our brains. As we discussed, this trait became accentuated by the belief in separation and autonomy that emerged in the 1700s in response to the stifling control of feudalism and the changes brought about by the Industrial Revolution. The reductionist view that resulted cemented the notion that dividing the world into little pieces helps us understand and control our environment.

Albert Einstein once observed that humans are part of the whole we call the "universe" but that we experience thoughts and feelings as something separate from the rest – a kind of optical illusion of the mind. We create the separation because putting boundaries between things allows us to categorize them as different from something else. We can, for example, distinguish trees from bushes and foreigners from our own people.

After we categorize something we can measure it. Trees are this high and include these properties, and bushes are smaller and have different characteristics. Foreigners look and act this way. Our people look and behave differently.

From these measurements, conclusions can be drawn. Trees have more economic worth than bushes. The values held by foreigners are inferior to those held by our people. Each step in the process generates more knowledge, we believe, which increases our capacity to control conditions around us.

Although helpful in many ways, if we are not aware of what we are doing this approach poses grave dangers. When we continually distinguish one thing from another our attention becomes focused on objects that can be easily seen and measured, such as the profit generated in our business, or the board feet of timber available in a forest. But in focusing on what can be measured, we often ignore the difficult to distinguish but nevertheless very real interconnections and feedbacks occurring between those things that make them what they are.

Even worse, every time we draw a line around something we create an opposite. The concept of "tall" can exist only if there is also a "short." A thing has value only if something else does not.[31] But the Earth's social, ecological, and climatic systems know nothing about the separations we humans have created in an attempt to understand and control our external environment. It is biologically impossible to separate a tree from the processes that sustain it, just as there is no way to separate the human mind from the human body.

Every divide we make, however, runs the risk of becoming a war zone because the more we separate things into different entities, the more hazards we see everywhere that must be constrained or conquered. Disharmony becomes the norm.[32] This is the origin of much of the injury we humans are causing to the Earth's climate and the natural environment.

The divides we make also cause great personal suffering. The relatively rapid shift from the survivalist "Me" focus of hunters and gatherers to the "We" collectiveness of clans, shows that humans are inherently social beings. The human brain has much larger and more elaborate frontal lobes than other organisms. Our larger brain provides us with an important evolutionary advantage: the capacity to problem-solve. But our brain size did not evolve merely in response to interactions with the natural environment. The many interactions we had with other humans was also a major contributor.[33]

From birth onward we thrive only when we are in relationships with others.[34] A sense of belonging to a larger group is essential to feeling good about ourselves and to our physical and emotional well-being. When we believe we exist as independent, separate entities, we deny that reality and cause ourselves great suffering.

Inequality of wealth provides a powerful example of the personal harm that results from the divides we create. When great disparities exist in wealth and incomes, as they do in the U.S., UK, and some other Western nations, health, and social problems can become extreme. This is not due merely to the fact that the poor have less access to decent food, housing, or medical care, although these factors are important. The more important issue is that because humans are inherently social creatures, our behavior is often driven by the fear of social disapproval and competition for higher status. The larger the gaps in income and wealth, the more pressure people feel to appear successful because they don't want others to look down on them. Fear of looking and feeling inferior often leads to loneliness and isolation, which drives people to behave in ways that undermine their health and well-being.[35]

When people feel separated they also experience higher rates of depression and anxiety, as well as more frequent heart problems, strokes, cancer, and other illnesses and diseases.[36] At its extreme, people become desperate for a sense of belonging. If the need is strong enough, people may join any group that will have them, including extremists that engage in wanton violence or thoughtlessly damage the environment. Violence is frequently a desperate attempt to gain respect.

People who feel deeply connected with other people, on the other hand, are happier and more fulfilled. They also have fewer emotional and physical problems. Thus, integration with others is essential for human well-being.[37]

We now see that we have over-consumed the Earth's resources and degraded many of its life-giving natural systems by separating ourselves from them. We have made it acceptable to dominate, exploit, and harm other people by creating boundaries that classify humans that live outside of the geographic, religious, ethnic, or political boundaries we have established as strangers, threats, and enemies. When we create these types of partitions we feel justified in ignoring the need to control our emotions, speech, and behavior. Much of the personal suffering we experience also results from the divisions we have created in our minds.

Once again, these partitions are myths. They don't exist in the real world. Our minds have created them merely as a way to make sense of, and influence, our external environment.

What you see in the world is in large part shaped by your assumptions and beliefs. Your thinking, in turn, influences how you interact with everything around you. If you, and the organizations you participate in, desire to begin the journey from "Me" to "We" and thrive in the difficult times ahead, you must abandon your fictional belief in separateness and make a commitment to see the integrated nature of the systems you are embedded within. You must become aware of the context in which you exist.

Systems can be difficult to quantity. But you can map them. Drawing maps of the social, economic, and ecological systems you are part of can be a fun and helpful way to expand your awareness of systems. Numerous examples of how to draw systems maps can be found on the web.[38]

When you make the commitment to see the systems you are part of an amazing journey will begin that can lead to a progressively deeper understanding of who you are as a person, as a member of the organizations you participate in, and as one of the many organisms on planet Earth. As numerous other people and organizations make this commitment, the world will take a step closer toward the "second-order" change required to overcome our past excesses, adjust to the demands of the 21st century, and begin to think and act sustainably.

But seeing the systems you are part of is only a first step in the transition from "Me" to "We." You must now look deeper and understand how to think about the consequences of your outdated thinking and behavior on those systems.

3
The second commitment
Be accountable for all the consequences of your actions

"We reap what we sow." This timeless proverb means we determine our future by what we do in the present. There is no way to avoid this natural law. We cannot plant seeds of one kind and expect to reap fruits of a different type. Wise people throughout the ages have told us that this is so.

Science has described this principle as well. Newton's Third Law of Motion says that "For every action there is an opposite and equal reaction." If we toss a stone into the air, it will fall to Earth every time. When we push over the first of a row of dominoes it will fall on the next, which will tumble onto the next and, eventually, cause the entire chain to collapse. Our planet is composed of interlocking webs of systems, so almost everything we do today has a consequence of some type, somewhere, at some point in time. This is the **Law of Cause and Effect**.

This natural law of sustainability is closely connected to the **Law of Interdependence** because it describes the consequences that occur when we fail to see and care for the Earth's social and ecological systems of which we are part.

Most people know that cause and effect exists. A young child grasps what happens when ice cream is left out of the freezer for too long. Adults know that driving too fast causes accidents. Yet those of us who grew up in the U.S., UK or other Western nations were raised in societies that promote the notion of separation and extreme individualism. Personally, and organizationally, we tend to focus almost exclusively on our own needs and wants – on "Me" – and deny, discount, or ignore the many ways in which our actions might affect the many systems we are part of – the broader "We" that makes life possible and worthwhile.

However, grasping what is truth and what is illusion about how we view the world and lead our lives is essential if we are to successfully address today's interlinked challenges. Understanding the relationship between cause and effect is a necessary step in the process. How often do you personally consider all of the possible direct, indirect, and non-linear effects of your behavior on the systems of which you are part? How often does your organization consider the full range of consequences of its activities?

If it is not your standard practice to continually strive to understand how you and the organizations you are involved with affect the systems you are embedded within, great distress will come to the planet, other people, and you, as always happens when a natural law is ignored. **The second commitment you and the organizations you are involved with must make to realize the shift from "Me" to "We" that is essential to resolving today's many crises, is to be accountable for *all* of the consequences of your actions.**

Five common erroneous views about cause and effect often exist:

- We assume one-way causality instead of feedback loops and thus fail to account for non-linear consequences.

- We underestimate or ignore inherent time delays between cause and effect.
- We respond to symptoms rather than addressing root causes.
- We focus on daily events rather than long-term patterns.
- We assume that the whole of a system will be improved by optimizing its parts.

As a result of these flawed perspectives, what we get from our actions is often quite different from what we expect.

The first erroneous belief about cause and effect is that the connection between a stimulus and its response is immediate, obvious, and always runs in the same direction. We often misinterpret Newton's principle in this way. As we frequently learn through the school of hard knocks, this simple straight-line thinking does not always match reality. Time and again, the relationship between a cause and its effects is indirect, not obvious, and runs in bewildering directions. Our failure to acknowledge this leads to reckless decisions and behavior.

To illustrate this point let's use a simplistic example focused on a social system. In order to feel superior you make a quick, modest, off-the-cuff criticism of a co-worker – call her Julie – and expect her response to be equally small, direct, and rapid. However, rather than responding as you thought, Julie is likely to outwardly smile and feign acceptance while internally harboring feelings of resentment that, over time, build to the point where the working relationship becomes completely fractured.

A second outcome of our mistaken thinking about cause and effect is our inability to consider that the consequences of our actions might not appear until long after the original cause has disappeared. Our failure to account for delays in the systems we are part of leads us to repeat the same dysfunctional behavior over and over because we don't immediately see the effects. If Julie fails to quickly voice her displeasure with your ridicule, you are likely to repeat the behavior, which will only reinforce her feelings of resentment.

Our failure to account for delays also leads to confusion between symptoms and root causes, which oftentimes divert attention away from fundamental solutions. Due to growing tension in your relationship, you might start to argue with Julie over inconsequential issues, which sidetracks the two of you from dealing with the real problem – Julie's resentment over your previous critical comments.

Sometimes a problem goes on for so long that it becomes difficult to establish what is the cause and what is the effect. This murkiness allows us to deny responsibility for our actions. Due to her repressed anger, Julie might direct a nasty comment at you, prompting another criticism from you, which triggers a vicious cycle of anger followed by ridicule. The original cause is all but lost in the escalating warfare, and you are absolved from any responsibility for initiating the rift in the relationship.

Our belief that daily crises can be resolved with quick fixes is another erroneous view about cause and effect. Although much of Western society is fixated on instant results, they typically make no real difference in our well-being, and frequently make things worse in the long run. That's because they ignore the deeper long-term problems that generate the daily crises in the first place. If you try to gloss over the underlying tension in your relationship by suddenly being super-nice, Julie is likely to become suspicious of your motives, making it even more difficult to talk about the root cause of her anger.

Our addiction to quick fixes and short-term success leads to another mistaken idea – that the whole of a system will be improved by optimizing its parts. Reality proves just the opposite. Optimizing individual parts of any ecological or social system in isolation normally reduces the performance of the overall system. When you ridiculed Julie to make yourself feel superior, the entire relationship broke down.

Every system has limits. When a part or a linkage is pushed beyond its threshold, the whole system can break down or collapse. Maximizing one aspect of a social or ecological system diminishes the whole because the feedback mechanisms that maintain the delicate balance among its elements and interactions are pushed beyond their limits. The complete breakdown of your relationship with Julie indicates that your ridicule overwhelmed the limits of her psychological defense mechanisms.

Does your personal way of thinking account for these surprising complexities? Does your organization regularly try to foresee the immediate and delayed, direct, indirect and non-linear effects of your actions? Do you and the organizations you participate in account for the possibility that if you go too far you might push the systems you are part of past their limits and cause them to flip into utterly new undesirable conditions, or even collapse? If the answer to these questions is "No," then time and again your behavior will give birth to startling and often unwelcome social, environmental, and personal consequences.

Let us examine how our failure to grasp the fundamentals of cause and effect is transforming the core systems of the Earth we discussed in the previous chapter.

Cause and effect and the climate

Our defective thinking is acutely altering the largest and most important system of concern to humans, the one involving the Sun and the Earth. Because no obvious consequences immediately appeared, our predecessors never considered the possibility that, after a delay, the effects of burning coal, oil, and gas to produce energy and clearing forests for agriculture would push the

Earth's climate system beyond its limits into a new, undesirable (from a human perspective) state. Many people today continue to think this way.

The concentration of carbon dioxide produced by our use of fossil fuels and other greenhouse gases has rapidly increased in the Earth's atmosphere. They are the largest direct cause of global climate disruption and the impacts result both from the amount of emissions and the speed at which they have increased. The gases humans have added to the atmosphere have enhanced the heat-trapping capacity of the blanket of greenhouse gases that naturally surround the Earth. As a result of exceeding the limits of the natural greenhouse effect, after a delay of well over a century, an energy imbalance has been created. More heat is collecting near the surface of the Earth than is escaping into space. This imbalance is what is disrupting the Earth's climate system.

Alterations to the Earth's forests and landscapes are the other direct causes of global climate disruption. They result from the same failure to account for cause and effect that lead to excessive greenhouse gases. When we cut down forests for lumber or convert them to farmland, carbon dioxide is directly released into the atmosphere. Because the cooling effect of vegetation is lost, part of the climate's self-regulating mechanism is weakened. Deforestation and other land use changes have contributed more than 20% of today's climate disruption by releasing carbon dioxide and reducing the Earth's capacity to sequester greenhouse gases.

The consequences of the disruption to the Earth's climate system are already significant. Surface temperatures have risen by 1°C above pre-industrial levels. Warming will increase by another 1°C, and might even rise as much as 6.4°C, which would be catastrophic for humans, unless atmospheric greenhouse gases are rapidly stabilized and eventually reduced to levels that existed prior to the Industrial Revolution.[39]

More extreme weather is one of the adverse effects of rising temperatures. Warmer temperatures have increased the amount of water vapor in the air by about 4%. The added moisture is being squeezed out in concentrated outpourings, leading to more frequent intense rainstorms and catastrophic floods around the globe.[40] The frequency and intensity of heat waves is also now outstripping record lows around the world by a 2 to 1 ratio.[41] In addition, the percentage of regions around the world experiencing extreme drought has more than doubled in the past 30 years.[42] A hotter global climate generates weird regional and local weather patterns.

Another tragic consequence of global climate disruption is sea-level rise. The oceans are absorbing much of the Earth's added warmth. Things expand when heated and rising temperatures have expanded the oceans. Melting ice sheets and glaciers will accelerate sea-level rise. Coastal flooding and higher storm surges will damage roads, homes, and other infrastructure, contaminate freshwater drinking supplies, and force millions of people worldwide to migrate to higher ground.

These are some of the early effects of global climate disruption. Disastrous surprises are also certain in the future. Our failure to understand or accept that we are pushing the Earth's climate system beyond its limits every time we turn on the lights, use electronic devices, drive vehicles, or in other ways use or burn fossil fuels and denude forests, is a matter of life and death for billions of people.

Cause and effect and the biosphere

The Earth's biosphere is another essential system that has been significantly harmed by our failure to understand cause and effect. As with global climate disruption, we have failed to grasp or acknowledge that some of the consequences of our actions on the planet's ecosystems and organisms might be immediate and obvious, and others are likely to be delayed and hard to see. We have also failed to consider that the cumulative effect of our actions might push the biosphere beyond its limits into altogether new and dangerous territory.

From our earlier discussion you know that each organism, no matter how small, plays an important role in the biosphere by influencing some other organism or process. Organisms affect, and are affected by, the continual exchange of energy and materials flowing through the Earth's ecosystems. They respond to a dynamic environment established, in part, by the organisms themselves. The life and death of organisms also affects the climate system and the climate affects organisms. Indeed, the Earth functions very much like a living system.

Continued degradation and loss of the organisms and interactions that make up the Earth's biosphere would be tragic. These systems produce and sustain the water we drink, the soils that grow our crops, and the air that we breathe. They are the source of food for us and all other organisms. Almost half of the world's economy is directly derived from biological resources. The Earth's natural assets are especially important to the poor, who directly rely on them for most of their food and material needs.

Unfortunately, we have failed to grasp the importance of sustaining the biosphere. We are in the midst of a mass extinction event equal in size to the one that eliminated the dinosaurs 65 million years ago. Natural forces wiped out the dinosaurs. We are the cause of today's extinctions. Many species are now disappearing 1,000 times faster than the normal background rate of extinction. A warming climate will add to the loss of biodiversity.

Rapidly increasing ocean acidification, also caused by our emission of carbon dioxide, will accelerate biological extinctions. The ocean naturally absorbs carbon dioxide. Under the world's current emissions path, by the middle of the 21st century ocean acidity is likely to increase by 150%. The rise will happen too quickly for many marine organisms to adapt, leading to a dramatic loss of marine biodiversity and fisheries.

Humans are part of the Earth's biosphere. Our lives, and the lives of all other living beings on the planet, are completely dependent upon it. Our failure to control our behavior and stay within the limits of these systems is generating self-inflicted mortal wounds.

Governments around the world have focused on ways to reduce the emission of greenhouse gases and prevent deforestation with the goal of avoiding global climate calamity. Although well-intentioned, they often confuse cause and effect. Greenhouse gas emissions and the depletion of ecosystems and biodiversity are merely symptoms of much deeper problems, which include booming population growth, technological capacity, and material consumption. These forces are driven by our erroneous assumptions and beliefs about how the planet functions and our role in it.

Two hundred years ago about one billion people inhabited the Earth. In 2011 the global population passed seven billion. The U.S. population more than tripled in the past century from about 76 million in 1900 to more than 300 million today, and Europe added 500 million people as well. The Earth's biosphere is being pushed beyond its limits by this massive swell of humanity. Yet few of us think about this when bringing a child into the world.

Our technological capacity has also exploded. It was just a little over 100 years ago that most people lived an agrarian lifestyle. Wagons pulled by horses and oxen were the primary source of transportation. Oil lamps, wood stoves, and steam provided most of the light, heat, and power. In Western nations today, gas-powered vehicles rapidly move huge numbers of people and goods, and giant cranes and bulldozers excavate tons of raw materials at a time. Centralized power plants provide electricity for cooking and heating. Our ability to extract and process more and more minerals, metals, and other natural resources at faster rates is far greater than at any other time in human history.

Consumption has rapidly increased as our population and technological capacity have expanded. In the U.S. in 1900 about 161 million metric tons of materials were consumed. By 2000, total consumption had grown to well over 3 billion metric tons.[43] Similar increases occurred in Europe.

Energy is needed to power society and fossil fuels provide more than three-quarters of the total energy consumed worldwide today. Petroleum leads the way with a bit less than 50% of total global energy consumption. North America is the largest consumer of fossil fuels, using almost a quarter of world resources.

Another way to think about our current consumption levels is that we are already using over 140% of the Earth's resources and ability to absorb our waste and impacts. If everyone in the world used the same amount of material as western Europeans, three additional Earth's would be needed. If everyone worldwide used the same amount as North Americans, seven additional planets would be needed.[44] Because we believe we exist independently from how the planet functions, few of us think about this when we go shopping or hop in our car.

We can now see that although greenhouse gas emissions and deforestation are the most direct causes of global climate disruption and damage to the biosphere, they are merely symptoms of much deeper causes, which are exponential growth in the human population, technological capacity, and resource consumption. These forces result from flawed assumptions and beliefs that prevent us from constraining our behavior. Trying to control the symptoms of these more fundamental drivers, including greenhouse gas emissions and deforestation, although important, is merely a band-aid. Few governments are willing to tackle these politically hot issues, so they continue to treat the symptoms rather than the root causes.

How is it that we cannot see these realities?

We have been told that competition is the primary driver of behavior in all organisms, and that human behavior is largely driven by an inherent desire to maximize self-interest. We therefore accept the idea that we should pursue our own personal and organizational desires and material gain without concern for the limits and feedbacks embedded within the ecological and social systems of the planet we are part of. Our tendency to create divisions between things in order to understand and control our environment reinforces this thinking. If each element and process functions separately, there is no need to worry about the possibility that our actions might, after a delay, trigger a string of undesirable cascading consequences. Just pursue your own needs and interests and everything will work out for the best.

The erroneous nature of these views should now be obvious. We failed to understand that organisms restrain their behavior in order to cooperate with each other just as much as they compete. Cooperation is evident in multicellular organisms, from nematodes to humans, all the way down to single-celled organisms such as bacteria and fungi. Because we thought only about our own immediate needs and desires, we failed to consider how our activities would, after a delay, break down the mutually supportive interactions occurring throughout the Earth's climate and biosphere. The consequences are far more pervasive than we ever imagined. By maximizing our own interests over all other systems on the planet, rather than enhancing the common good, we have crippled the planet's capacity to support life, including us.

We have been living in a dream world, unable or unwilling to see how the world actually functions. Our illusions have led us to ignore cause and effect in ways that are disastrous for the planet, for each of us, and for our organizations as well.

Cause and effect and social systems

Our erroneous thinking about cause and effect has significant implications for the social systems we are embedded within as well. To survive, we humans require a deep level of trust in the strength of our relationships. When we trust others, a sense of closeness develops. We realize that our destiny is connected to other people. Strong social systems keep us healthier and allow us to live longer.[45]

In contrast, when our trust level is low we become suspicious and establish barriers between ourselves and other people. Relationships break down and we become pessimistic and defensive. Self-centered behavior often results, which harms others, but ultimately damages us the most.

The economy is a case in point. Many economists, business executives, and politicians tell us that government regulation is "bad" while, at the same time, huge corporations, Wall Street, and other private power brokers control much of our lives through the power they hold over the economy and their capacity to shape the political process to ensure that it supports their interests. These people continuously promote the notion that, if left alone, the invisible hand of the market will always work things out for the best. There is no need, therefore, to worry about other people or ecological processes. Just pursue your own material interests and society will be better off. Experience after experience, however, proves this belief to be categorically wrong.

The behavior of Wall Street brokers and investment banks that led to the financial crash of 2008 is one of many recent examples. The people leading these companies separated the world into "us" and "everyone else." This led the executives to conclude that they were the smartest kids on the block because people considered to be different are almost always seen as inferior.

The financial wizards used predatory, unethical, and illegal practices to con the people they deemed less important into buying questionable mortgages and other financial "products," while the bankers raked in millions for themselves. People at the middle and lower income levels responded to the wealth they saw accumulating at the top with a combination of envy and fear of being left behind. They bought mortgages they could not afford, took on extensive debt, and ate into their savings to make the payments. Of course, after a delay of a few years, the system suddenly collapsed. By 2009 over $14 trillion in wealth held by U.S. households was wiped out, a total equal to the entire US GDP in 2008.

Wall Street, the mortgage industry, and the government agencies that were established to oversee them forgot that short-term profits do not guarantee long-term successes. To the contrary, quick massive profits usually indicate major imbalances in the financial system that lead to big trouble.

The traders and regulators also failed to acknowledge that all systems, financial or otherwise, have limits. When one group within the economy maximized their interests over all others, the checks and balances that maintained the interdependencies among the elements of the system were pushed beyond their threshold and eventually crumpled.

How many times do we have to see the damage done to a larger system by individual actors maximizing their own self-interest before we realize the fundamental flaws in the notions promoted by thinkers in the 1700s, and by so many others today? They may have made sense 250 years ago when society was reacting to the rigid control of feudalism, few people roamed the land, trade occurred mostly at the local level, and human technologies and consumption had modest environmental impacts. But conditions have fundamentally changed and today this thinking and behavior leads to ruin.

Cause and effect and organizations

A proper understanding of cause and effect is also critical to the success of any organization. If people don't agree on the likely consequences of specific actions, big trouble usually results.

Imagine, for instance, that you work in a business that is struggling to make a profit. Your CEO announces that the company is going to launch an extensive marketing campaign to increase sales. Unless you and your co-workers agree that you can handle a major rapid increase in production, pumping up sales is likely to overwhelm everyone, cause production delays, lead to mistakes and defective products, and eventually cause even more financial distress.

Oftentimes, organizations pursue a quick fix for a problem and continue with business-as-usual after visible signs of trouble disappear. Following our example, your company launched an extensive marketing campaign when profits drop, believing that increased sales will enhance profits. Because the quick fix typically fails to resolve the root cause of the problem, after a delay, the original problem reappears, often in a slightly different form. Since the "solution" seemed to make the problem go away the previous time, the same fix is applied once again. Boosting sales at your fictional firm led to a bump in profits last time, so the company cranks up its marketing efforts again the next time profits drop.

After this dynamic is repeated a few times, organizations often become addicted to the quick fix. This makes it difficult, if not impossible, to address the root causes of trouble. Continuing with our example, a vicious cycle is triggered whereby the amplified marketing campaign exhausts employees and depletes the company's capital reserves, leaving insufficient funds to hire the new staff and buy the equipment needed to manufacture products in a timely manner without defects. Sales consequently drop again because customers eventually stop buying defective products, which further deplete the funds available to invest in new staff and equipment.

This example shows how important it is for the members of an organization to understand and agree on how cause and effect actually works. Without this knowledge, people will not know what activities to pursue and what to avoid.

Cause and effect and family and personal well-being

Too often, family members also forget that they reap what they sow. When a parent exerts overbearing authority on, withholds attention from, or depreciates a child, the youngster's self-esteem can be systematically destroyed. What appears at the time to the parent as inconsequential actions or comments can wound a child for life. Substance abuse is known as a family disease affecting children, spouses, brothers and sisters, as well as parents and other relatives of the user. Addiction often produces direct and indirect effects that impair one or more family member for decades. When we ignore cause and effect we can do great harm to our family systems.

We often fail to acknowledge that "what goes around comes around" applies to our internal mind–body systems as much as it does to external processes. A quarter of the U.S. population still smokes, almost as many people drink too much alcohol, and about 10% use illicit drugs.[46] The rates are roughly the same or in the case of smoking higher in Western Europe.[47]

Many people ignore or discount the physical, emotional, and psychological consequences of these activities, which can be quick and dramatic or appear only after a long delay. For example, the U.S. Surgeon General recently declared that even one

3 The second commitment

puff of a cigarette or one breath of second-hand smoke can cause a fatal heart attack.[48]

If we are lucky enough to avoid sudden death, after a delay of many years the stress on our bodies from smoking often leads to cancer or other diseases. Cigarette smoking causes almost 90% of the lung cancer deaths among men, and 80% among women. Smoking is also associated with cancer of the mouth, pharynx, larynx, bladder, stomach, kidneys, and pancreas and it is implicated in leukemia. We reap what we sow.

You undoubtedly consider yourself to be a thoughtful person. Your organization probably considers itself to be socially responsible. This suggests that you believe you can envision the consequences of your actions. But, be honest; is this really so? Is it your custom to personally consider *all* of the possible effects of your behavior? Does your organization *always* seek to account for *all* of the potential consequences of its activities throughout its entire value chain? Do you consider how the activities of society as a whole can build up, feed off each other, and produce impacts that cannot be predicted by the actions of any single person or organization?

For instance, have you taken the time to understand the science that clearly shows that the Earth's climate and biosphere have been pushed to their limits and are now on the brink of collapse? Have you given careful thought to what the consequences of those breakdowns might mean for you and your family, the organizations you are involved with, and civilization as a whole? Have you considered how chaotic and difficult the next decades will be due to the fact that we have hit the planet's social and ecological limits? If you have not thought deeply about these issues, you are not accurately thinking about cause and effect.

Although no one can be held responsible for accidental harm, we are each responsible for the injury that occurs if we act thoughtlessly or negligently by failing to consider the possible consequences of our actions on the climate, biosphere, or social systems we are part of. We are also responsible for damage originating elsewhere if we have the capacity to help reduce or prevent it, but fail to act. You, and the organizations you participate in, must seek to be constantly aware of *all* of the possible direct and indirect, immediate and long-term, close-by and geographically distant upshots of your behavior on other people and the natural environment.

As with systems, cause-and-effect relationships can be difficult to quantify. But they can be mapped. Tools such as "Fishbone" diagrams can help you understand the possible consequences of your actions.[49]

For most of us, recognizing the effects of our actions requires much more than a few slight improvements. It requires "second-order change," meaning that you must live much more mindfully than ever before. At home you must consider the impacts on the ecological and social systems you are part of every time you set your thermostat, turn on a TV, drive your car, buy a product, toss out the garbage, or consider having a child. At work you must think about the consequences of your entire organization's value-chain, starting with whether your goods and services help resolve today's pressing problems or whether they promote unnecessary consumption and fossil fuel use, thus contributing to ecological and social breakdown. If your products serve an essential need, you must then consider the quantity and methods used to extract and process raw materials, as well as your transportation, marketing, manufacturing, packaging, transportation, energy use, and waste practices, how your customers use and dispose of the product, and much more.

Becoming more attentive in this way will not prevent you from acting. People who make the effort to be mindful of the consequences of their behavior are more keenly interested in things occurring around them. They are more open to unexpected opportunities and find it easier to side-step events and avoid personal behaviors that might delay engagement in the world. The blindness caused by lack of awareness, on the other hand, leads to barriers that prevent full engagement.

Awareness is everything. The more mindful you become of the potential effects of your actions, the greater your awareness will become. Like the other commitments involved with the shift from "Me" to "We," as other people and organizations make a similar commitment our society will increase its understanding of the implications of our past and current practices, and take another step toward true sustainability.

4
The third commitment
Abide by society's most deeply held universal principles of morality and justice

Imagine, for a moment, that a genie suddenly whisks you away from your everyday life and makes you the world's most powerful decision-maker. At your fingertips is the most up-to-date information about the planet's economic, social, and environmental conditions. You can use that data to make any type of decision you want about how resources and wealth should be allocated and how things should function.

But there is a catch. The genie has also given you amnesia. You cannot remember your social status, nationality, gender, ethnicity, religious affiliation, how much money you have, or even who your parents or family are. Consequently, you don't know what the effects of your decisions will be on you or your loved ones because you don't know who you are or where you live.[50]

Under these conditions, would you think and act the same way as you do now? Would you, for example, use as much energy, consume as many resources, or generate as much solid waste and greenhouse gas emissions as you do today? Would you seek to accumulate as much personal wealth or power?

Remember that you might actually reside among the poor in Africa, Asia, or the Pacific where sea-level rise, extreme heat waves, droughts, floods, diseases, and food shortages generated by human-induced climate disruption and biodiversity extinctions are currently most extreme. Or, you might live in a low-income area or among the infirm, elderly, women, children, or a community of color in the U.S. and Europe that face similar threats. Would you continue to think and behave as you do now?

Not likely. Instead, you would undoubtedly adopt a decision-making process similar to the universal moral principle known as the "Golden Rule" which says: "Treat others as you would like them to treat you." In other words, you would no longer focus only on your own wants and needs but instead consciously choose to see things through the eyes of people all over the world because those "others" might include you! You would shift your perspective from "Me" to "We."

As far-fetched as this scenario seems, it describes the reality of the world we live in today. Although you might never have omnipotent power, no matter who you are, or where you live, you can be negatively affected by the actions of anyone on the planet at any time. Similarly, your activities, and those of the organizations you are a member of, can affect people around the globe as well as all future generations in surprising ways. To ensure your own well-being, you must therefore make decisions that enhance the well-being of everyone else.

Committing to seeing the social and ecological systems you are part of, and accounting for all of the ways your activities are likely to affect those systems, are necessary conditions for the shift from "Me" to "We." But this is only a start. You must now decide on the moral principles that will guide your response to those consequences. What moral standards will you hold yourself to as you respond to the breakdown of the climate and biosphere and the social and economic crises they trigger? What principles of morality and justice will your organization base its activities on?

In today's over-crowded, over-consumed, over-polluted, and over-heating world, morally just behavior is more essential than ever before. That's because moral action is not based on philosophy or good intentions. It is based on real-world consequences. This is the **Law of Moral Justice**. This natural law of sustainability says that morally just behavior is imperative now because at this moment in history, our survival requires exemplary levels of human self-control, cooperation, and principled action. Without this, everyone will suffer, including you and me.

Although instinctual drives and the capacity to reason shape human behavior, the moral precepts we hold ourselves to determine how those processes play out. **The third commitment you and the organizations you are involved with must make to realize the shift from "Me" to "We" that is essential to resolving today's many crises, is to abide by society's most deeply held universal principles of morality and justice.**

Consciously choosing to practice moral justice is a "second-order change" that can guide your response to the adversity resulting from the collapse of the planet's social and ecological systems. It will help you plot a route through the tough times ahead with integrity and honor, while serving as a model for others. Practicing moral justice will also help your organization become part of the solution rather than part of the problem, and so thrive in the future.

Morality and justice

Morality involves answers to age-old questions such as which human behaviors are right and which are wrong, which are fair and unfair, and what our duties and obligations are to other people. When humans survived on their own in the wild, they did not need to consider these questions. But every since people banded together in groups, they have been forced to decide how to live together. This requires a mixture of self-imposed internal constraints on the selfish and aggressive aspects of our personalities, and the magnification of altruistic traits that bring forth caring and cooperation behaviors. The moral axioms we adhere to determine the weight we give to these different qualities. They also frame the social norms, laws, and principles of justice our society adopts to govern how people treat each other. Indeed, morality is one of humanities noblest achievements.

In Western nations nowadays, most people don't seem to spend much time thinking about these issues. Our belief in extreme individualism, born from ideas that emerged three centuries ago, has shifted the focus of Western morality away from concerns about how we should relate to others, to what is best for each of us personally.

In its most positive form we are left with a moral perspective that promotes individual rights. This perspective has led to much advancement. It has, for instance, provided the moral and legal justification for civil rights, women's rights, and many other social movements, as well as protection of property rights and the right to honest profit. The world has seen the tragic consequences that occur for people and the natural environment in societies without such individual rights, such as those that existed behind the Iron Curtain in the 20th century.

However, when we consider the far-reaching consequences of the individualistic view of morality and justice on the overstressed systems we, and our organizations are part of, it becomes clear that this view is insufficient. Our focus on individual rights, for example, leads us to extend the right not to be harmed by the actions of others only to ourselves. People, and entire cultures, living elsewhere in the world do not have a similar right to be protected from the effects of our activities.

The focus on individual rights also fails to protect the rights of future generations who will inherit what we leave for them, but have no say in what we do today.

Our "Me First and Only" view of morality has, in addition, led to a deep loss of personal and organizational integrity and honor. Without a commitment to abide by long held codes of morality and justice we, and our organizations, easily sink into selfish, narcissistic and destructive behaviors.

These problems exist because our individualist view of morality leads us to take a non-judgmental approach to human behavior. Instead of calling out and opposing injustice, we see morality in strictly relative terms, with no absolute rights or wrongs. We believe each person should be free to abide by the moral principles and sense of justice that best fit their lifestyle.

Most of us use a number of psychological tricks to justify our non-judgmental perspective of morality. For instance, we can recast our destructive behavior as virtuous. Or, we distance ourselves from the pain we inflict on others by minimizing our personal responsibility. We are also skilled at altering the way we think about harm itself, and can become experts at blaming the victims and declaring them to be unworthy of humane consideration.[51]

But justice cannot be served through this approach. After all, white Americans once saw slavery as beneficial to their lifestyle and made it the law in the U.S. Apartheid was once the law of the land in South Africa. Many other unjust practices and laws have existed throughout history. Horrific things almost always happen when people promote their personal and organizational self-interest without a sound moral foundation.[52] As with so many other views today that are based on the beliefs in separation and extreme individualism, the emphasis has become misplaced. We have become blind to the moral implications of our behavior. No human right is secure under these conditions.

The focus on individual rights comes up short because it neglects the duties and responsibilities we have to treat other people just as we want other people to treat us: fairly and humanely. It also fails to put our obligations to protect the basis of all life – the climate and biosphere – ahead of the rights of human to manipulate it for material gain. Rights and duties are both important. But they are not the same. Without a sound moral foundation focused on the duties we have to maintain the ecological and social systems that exist on the planet, it is clear that an individualist view of morality will not make for a just or sustainable society.

The shift from "Me" to "We" required to guide us through the rocky times ahead and eventually resolve our troubles requires that each of us, and each of our organizations, must affirm and abide by the moral duties and obligations that all human rights, justice, liberty – and, indeed, survival – depend on.

Sources of morality

Even though an individualistic moral perspective dominates today, most of humanity has, throughout history, declared certain behaviors to be right and others to be wrong. These moral principles have been derived from three sources: evolution; human reasoning; and religion.

Scientists studying our closest primate relatives have observed behaviors that are very similar to the moral behaviors seen in human groups. For example, chimpanzees exhibit behaviors that appear to include altruism, sympathy, sharing, fairness, and moral disapproval. Capuchin monkeys have demonstrated a strong aversion to inequity in their group relations. This strongly suggests that the moral sense of fairness and justice are, like many other human behaviors, instinctual reactions that are deeply rooted in emotional responses that are at least partly embedded in our genes.[53]

Our ability to reason adds another layer to our instinctual desire for moral behavior. It allows us to override the powerful affects of our emotions by seeing that the interplay between the laws of interdependence and cause and effect require people to treat each other with compassion and respect because we must protect the welfare of others in order to ensure our own well-being. We thus have the capacity to extend our moral sentiments beyond our immediate family and friends to other people, whole cultures, and even to the natural environment.

Throughout much of history the world's religions have been the primary source of moral guidance for humans, and many people believe moral principles are a gift from God. No matter what the source may be, it is clear that moral precepts are not merely theoretical propositions. They are powerful motivators of human thinking, emotions, and behavior that shape our sense of integrity and well-being.

The two universal moral principles

A number of moral principles have existed throughout time. They can be condensed into two universal axioms.[54] The first is to "do no harm," which is the focus of this chapter. The second, "do good," will be discussed in the next chapter.[55]

Almost every religious and spiritual tradition, and every theory of moral philosophy, proclaims that whenever possible we should care for and help other people. If that is not possible, we should at least "do no harm." Thus, any activity that unjustifiably causes human suffering or death is morally wrong. The moral tenet to "do no harm" also includes the duty not to lie, steal, cheat, falsely accuse, or psychologically or emotionally abuse others. These obligations seek to constrain the self-centered and aggressive "Me" focused aspects of our psyche. Self-control resulting from the application of the moral principle to "do no harm" is a human trait long known to generate a wide range of personal and social benefits. This moral precept is captured by the inverse of the Golden Rule: "Do not do to others what you would not want them to do to you."[56]

Historically, this moral axiom has been applied only to humans. However, the awareness that all life, including our own, exists only because of the Earth's climate and biosphere means that these systems must also be included in the axiom. To "do no harm" we must refrain from actions that undermine the health and vitality of the natural environment upon which all life, human and otherwise, depends.

We know that we need to "do no harm" if we are to live together in relative harmony with our families, neighbors, and others around the world. Our individualist view of morality, however, prevents us from seeing or passing judgment on the many ways in which our personal behaviors, and the activities of our businesses and governments today, constantly violate this universal moral precept. Let's examine some of the consequences of this failure.

The consequences of failing to 'do no harm'

As we have discussed, the most important system from a human perspective is the one involving the Sun and the Earth. The planet's climate system determines the health and well-being of all people and organisms. Yet, in large part due to human-generated greenhouse gases and massive deforestation, 20 million people were displaced by climate disruption-induced sudden onset disasters in 2008.⁵⁷ An estimated 350,000 human deaths are already occurring each year due to climate disruption and, in the absence of an aggressive response, by 2030 worldwide deaths will likely reach one million annually.⁵⁸ An additional 660 million people per year are expected to suffer physically, emotionally, or psychologically from disasters triggered by profound changes in the Earth's climate.⁵⁹

One of the most significant sources of suffering is the dramatic rise in warming-related disease and illness.⁶⁰ Water, air, insect-borne diseases and illnesses, and heart disease will increase. Mental health problems and heat-related illnesses will rise. Asthma rates will likely double and the asthma season will lengthen as the Earth warms.⁶¹

Truly, climate disruption puts the health of everyone at risk, but people living in poverty, the infirm, women, children, the elderly, and the obese are particularly vulnerable to these health effects.

Uncontrolled climate disruption also promises to cause a horrifying level of economic suffering. Already, it creates an estimated $150 billion in losses annually. By 2030, the total is expected to rise to between $275 and $340 billion annually due to market instabilities, sea-level rise, and the impacts of natural disasters.⁶² The costs of adapting to floods and climate impacts on health, food systems, and other resources are estimated to add another $120 to $510 billion annually.⁶³

These cost projections are undoubtedly low. Some economists have determined that the "social costs" of carbon have been undervalued by as much as 45 times. If this is accurate, the economic suffering caused by uncontrolled climate disruption is likely to be in the $ trillions annually.⁶⁴ Indeed, because our economy is merely a subset of the natural environment, without a dramatic change in direction, as climate disruption unfolds, the global economy will teeter on the brink of total collapse. Our inability to acknowledge or abide by the universal moral precept to "do no harm" and constrain human activities that disrupt the climate will cause millions to lose their jobs, living standards to drop, and poverty to skyrocket.

Although few citizens of the U.S. grasp this, people throughout the less developed regions of the world blame the U.S. for creating most of the climatic troubles that are causing tremendous suffering and death in their nations. They are especially angry at our continued unwillingness to help stabilize the climate by cutting our emissions. The U.S. is now viewed as a dishonorable nation. It has lost the respect of millions of people worldwide.

Our unwillingness to follow the moral precept of "do no harm" has also profoundly affected the Earth's biosphere, which is the system of next greatest importance to humans. The planet's intricate web of organisms and ecological processes provide the air we breathe, the food we eat, and the materials that support our economy. Shockingly, due to unsustainable land development, logging, farming, fishing, and other practices driven by the relentless pursuit of economic growth, almost a third of the known vertebrate species became extinct between 1970 and 2006. All over the world, natural habitats are in decline and genetic diversity is falling. The problem will worsen as global temperatures climb even higher.[65]

The human suffering caused by the breakdown of the biosphere is also disturbing. Ocean acidification caused by carbon dioxide emissions is destroying sea life, including the marine fisheries that millions of people worldwide rely on for jobs and 3.5 billion depend upon for their primary source of protein.[66] Furthermore, the loss of biodiversity will reduce our ability to obtain many types of medicines, food, fibers, water, and other resources that are essential for human life. The depletion and loss of these resources, combined with the economic costs of climate disruption, will result in appalling human suffering and death.

Moreover, our failure to abide by the universal moral precept to "do no harm" causes significant suffering for the people involved with the social systems we are part of. When we fail to control our selfish "Me" focused traits and act immorally, we often feel guilty, ashamed, unworthy, or embarrassed. These powerful emotions can cause us to defend ourselves by lashing out at others. Our reaction can escalate already tense situations into a cycle of conflict where as one party strikes at another, both see themselves as unworthy, and everyone's sense of shame increases.

People who have been treated as lesser humans because of their ethnic identity, for instance, often feel intense shame and anger and retaliate with aggressive and violent behavior. This dynamic can also be seen in a divorce, where one spouse feels ashamed or unworthy and lashes out at the other, who returns the insults, leading to a cycle of increasing acrimony.

When we fail to abide by our moral obligation to "do no harm" we also inflict a great deal of emotional and psychological pain on ourselves. Our lack of self-control leads to guilt and shame that causes us to think something is wrong with us. We often adopt dysfunctional inward-turning behaviors such as avoiding friends and family. Some people seek wealth, power, or perfection in order to avoid future shame. Others blame or disparage friends or strangers under the misguided hope that they will be lifted up by putting others down. While in the short run these behaviors might relieve some of the guilt, in the long run they only strengthen feelings of shame and worthlessness.

Duties of the moral precept 'do no harm'

It should now be clear that the failure to "do no harm" causes tremendous suffering and death for people across the globe, our organizations, and ourselves. The cumulative effects of these and other issues have led us into one of the most chaotic and challenging periods in human history. If we want to transition through the long period of turmoil we have now entered with as few wounds as possible and come out the other side in a more stable and sustainable condition, we must make a commitment to voluntarily impose on ourselves a clear set of moral standards that help us control our thinking, emotions, and behavior.

This code of thinking and behavior starts by acknowledging that it is every individual's birthright to live free from the consequences of destructive resource extraction practices, excessive consumption, toxicity, and greenhouse gases that produce climate disruption, ocean acidification, biodiversity loss, and their associated social and economic calamities. We must also acknowledge our moral obligation to protect the collective rights of groups and whole societies that have contributed little to today's environmental and social crises, but who suffer the most. In addition, we must recognize our obligation to protect our children and all future generations from diminished opportunities caused by our self-focused activities. Most importantly, we must accept our duty to put the protection of the Earth's natural systems that make all life possible above the rights of humans to manipulate it for pleasure or material gain.

These duties are natural expressions of the rights to life, liberty, and personal security, which are the universal human rights upon which all other rights depend. They are the duties that form the foundation for other widely recognized rights found in international law and practice, such the "precautionary principle." They are recognized in international treaties and are also clearly described in Article 3 of the Universal Declaration of Human Rights.[67] Even free-market ideology is based on the notion that people should be free to do as they wish as long as their activities do not infringe on the rights of others to do the same.[68]

The moral obligation to accept limits on human behavior

No concept of morality or justice is possible unless people accept that some limits are necessary on human behavior. The reality is that we accept limits all the time in order to live safely and securely. No one could set foot outside of their home without the risk of being assaulted unless laws and enforcement mechanisms existed to control aggressive behavior. No one would feel comfortable eating food produced by distant corporations without quality standards that prevent manufacturers from selling contaminated food. You would not even feel safe driving a vehicle without rules of the road because people would be free to travel in the opposite direction in your lane.

Yet we refuse to accept the need to live within limits when it comes to the planet's climate, biosphere, and social systems. Our belief in extreme individualism leads us to conclude that continuous economic growth and material acquisition are possible without pushing species and ecological process beyond their limits into a permanently degraded state. We see no reason to constrain our use of fossil fuels to avoid exceeding the limits of the climate. We deny there are limits to the amount of economic inequity that can exist in a society before widespread health and social problems occur. As with many other beliefs today, these are fantasies.

All systems have limits. When we push systems too far the feedback mechanisms that support their resiliency and integration break down and collapse. Psychologists know that the ability to limit our behavior, not unconstrained freedom, leads to greater happiness. The ability to control our thinking, emotions, and behavior increases our capacity to resist short-term temptations in favor of long-term benefits. People with good self-control are more able to form and maintain close relationships because they can take the time to see things from the perspective of others rather than causing rifts by impulsively giving in to self-focused or aggressive urges. They also tend to be more emotionally stable and suffer from fewer psychological problems such as anxiety, depression, or addiction than people with little self-control. Not surprisingly, self-control builds on itself. The more we exert, the greater our self-esteem becomes, which enhances our willpower.[69]

In addition, psychologists know that less choice, not more, increases contentment. Although this might seem like blasphemy to people who are wedded to the notion of unlimited choice resulting from the beliefs in separation and extreme individualism, the key is to understand what to limit and how it should be accomplished. Wisdom, peace of mind, and happiness arise from personal awareness that helps us see the great distress to others and ourselves that arises when we allow our aggressive and self-focused traits to run free. The more self-aware we are, the greater our capacity to express the self-focused and aggressive side of ourselves only when absolutely necessary. Thus, the more that we limit the circumstances under which we allow our selfish tendencies to be expressed, the wiser and happier we become.[70]

To make the shift from "Me" to "We" and transition to sustainable thinking and acting we must accept the moral obligation to constrain our "Me First and Only" impulses and live within the limits of our social and ecological systems.

The moral obligation to rise above 'us-versus-them' stereotyping

One of the requirements of living within the limits of our social and ecological systems is the need to see "in-group" versus "out-group" thinking for what it is: an illusion of the mind. Through evolution, humans developed "us-versus-them" thinking as a self-defense mechanism. As observed previously, in our hunter–gatherer years we learned to quickly categorize people, animals, and situations as safe or dangerous in order to avoid peril. Snap judgments and quick reactions were key to survival. By simplifying the world into fixed categories such as good or bad, friend or foe, we increased our capacity to rapidly decide if something we encountered should be avoided or embraced.

Although "us-versus-them" thinking helped our ancestors survive in the wild, it has outlived its usefulness. The habit of labeling people as "different" because they reside outside of the political boundaries we establish, look unusual, or have different personal traits or cultural norms leads us to quickly classify them as unworthy of the same type of consideration we give to "our own." In-group loyalty increases, while empathy is reduced, and animosity, exploitation, and abuse toward "outsiders" rises, even when they pose no threat. The more people believe their group is the most righteous, the greater their fanaticism.

This is a very dangerous dynamic given the interconnected nature of the world economy today, and the globalized consequences of the breakdown of the climate and biosphere. There is no "us" and "them" any longer. We are all in the same soup together. The growing suite of crises will impact everyone on the planet, but equally everyone will benefit from solutions.

To live within the limits of the planet's social and ecological systems and prevent unjustifiable suffering and death, we must become mindful of when we are engaged in the dynamic and limit the use of "us-versus-them" thinking. One way to accomplish this is to increase our exposure to people we have previously stereotyped. Researchers have found that mutual trust can grow and rapidly spread when people make direct contact with others.[71]

The point to remember is that there are no "others" when it comes to climate disruption and the degradation of the biosphere.

We must step outside the illusion of this mind-set and realize that now there is only "We."

The moral obligation to adopt means to resolve conflict peacefully

One of the most important implications of the need to live within limits and rise above "in-group" versus "out-group" thinking is the imperative to put a stop to the use of violence to resolve conflicts. Unless we establish peaceful ways to settle disputes, unprecedented levels of suffering and death will mark the future.

Even if we successfully reduce greenhouse gas emissions over the next decade, the legacy of emissions already concentrated in the atmosphere means that global temperatures are likely to rise close to, or beyond, 2°C. As temperatures inch toward that level, essential resources such as water will become increasingly scarce. Some regions of the world will become uninhabitable due to excessive heat and drought, repeated storm damage, sea-level rise, or the soaring costs of providing water, energy, food, and shelter. At the same time, the expanding global population will try to squeeze into ever-smaller areas of fertile, habitable land. Humans are more likely to revert to violence under conditions of crowding and resource scarcity – which are the exact conditions climate disruption will bring. To avoid calamity under these conditions, we must consciously undertake the difficult but doable task of developing mechanisms to control the individual and institutional human propensity toward learned violence.

Two words in the previous sentence – "doable" and "learned" – are important to this discussion. It is possible to prevent the use of violence to sort out quarrels because it is a learned cultural response.

Many people believe that humans are naturally violent. This is not true, at least not in the way we normally think about it. No evidence exists that we are innately violent. Instead, thousands of years of evolution have endowed humans with the predisposition to respond to perceived external threats with defensiveness and hostility that can escalate in intensity to the point where the threat is eliminated. As discussed, this trait is magnified when we create divides between "in-groups" composed of family and friends, and "out-groups" made up of others that we see as aliens and threats, and when we believe resources are scarce or we are crowded together.[72]

Those qualities, however, do not play out the same way in every human society. In some groups, such as a few South American nations and inner-city gangs in the U.S., violence towards others is common and even glorified. In others, such as the cultures of Denmark and Sweden, and religious orders such as the Amish or Buddhist communities, violence is rare and seen as a sign of personal weakness.[73] This shows that culture, not biology, determines the extent to which we humans behave violently to others.[74]

The deteriorating and overcrowded conditions of our planet mean that the learned rules of violent behavior that dominate a number of societies are now obsolete and must be abolished. We long ago left the era where disagreements can be settled by guns, bombs, or chemical agents. But to say that violence must be prevented does not mean it will disappear. Individually, we must use our capacity for awareness and rational thought to consciously establish internal psychological controls on characteristics that are biological in nature. We must also establish external cultural norms, as well as laws and political institutions that allow us to peacefully resolve discord and prevent others from using violence. A moral commitment to restraint and pacifism must become firmly embedded in our culture if we are to avoid incessant climate disruption and biosphere breakdown-induced harm to other people and ourselves.

The moral obligation to cut material and energy consumption

To live within limits and avoid the outbreak of violent behavior, every individual, household, and organization in Western nations has a moral obligation to dramatically reduce their consumption of raw materials and energy. We cannot prevent unjustifiable human suffering or death without cutting consumption because we have overshot the Earth's ecological limits and must make up for the excesses of the past.

Our economy operates today much like many governments – by growing a larger and larger debt. Although financial debt is substantial, by far our largest debt is ecological. We grow our economy only by drawing down the Earth's forests, oceans, water resources, biodiversity, atmosphere, and other sources of "natural capital." We believe we are generating wealth but in reality we are eating into our principal and getting poorer.

Left unchecked, the ecological debt we are creating will cause human suffering and death for centuries to come. We are lying to others and ourselves to believe otherwise. Wealthy consumers are also cheating people around the world out of their fair share of the planet's resources and stealing from future generations. To abide by the moral precept to "do no harm" we must acknowledge our indiscretions by reducing our material and energy consumption.

Public policies will be essential to achieving these ends. But even if our governments are unable to adopt or enforce meaningful limitations, each individual, household, and organization has a moral obligation to rapidly and significantly cut consumption.

One of the primary reasons for reducing consumption is that everyone on the planet has an equal right to emit some greenhouse gases into the Earth's atmosphere. This principle is firmly established in the UN's Framework Convention on Climate Change[75] which was endorsed by all Western nations, including the U.S. Western nations, however, and the U.S. in particular, have taken up far more than their fair share of the "atmospheric space" available for emissions. We must reduce our emissions to levels that avoid the worst of the climate crisis while also providing the "atmospheric space" needed by people in less developed nations to expand their economies and raise their citizens out of poverty.

We cannot substantially reduce emissions, however, without reducing our consumption of energy and raw materials. Why? In Chapter 2 I discussed how human impacts on the environment are the result of a combination of the size of the population, consumption, and technological capacity. All three factors contribute to today's crises, and all three must be addressed to reduce those problems.

Programs to limit population always seem to trigger intense political backlash and thus become non-starters. Because our economic system is predicated on the need for continual growth, proposals to limit consumption are also usually quickly dismissed. With population and consumption taken off the table, the only solution we are left with is technological changes.

This is a mistake. Although new technologies will be essential for the transition to a sustainable economy, technological solutions alone cannot solve the climate crises. To the contrary, many new technologies actually reinforce the problems they were designed to solve by increasing the global demand for raw materials and energy.

Fossil fuels provide the vast majority of the energy in Western nations. Rapid cuts in energy consumption are therefore the most direct and, indeed, only viable way to quickly slash emissions.

Some of the initial priorities should be residential and commercial buildings, vehicles, air, and other forms of transportation, appliances, and electronic equipment. Many tools and methods are available for these purposes.

The good news is that we can rapidly slash energy consumption in ways that actually improve, not diminish, our quality of life. That's because we waste a whopping amount of energy. Lawrence Livermore National Laboratory found that 58% of all energy produced in the U.S. is wasted, including over 65% of the energy produced for electricity and almost 75% of the energy produced for transportation. About 20% of the energy generated to power industry, and 20% of the energy we use in residential and commercial buildings is also wasted.[76]

An analysis by McKinsey & Company in 2007 found that energy consumption in the U.S. could be reduced by 7–28% by 2030 compared to 2005 through changes in behavior and the use of existing and rapidly emerging practices and technologies with no real change in lifestyle. Forty per cent of the reductions could be achieved with little to no costs or even produce a net economic benefit.[77] Many other studies have reached similar conclusions. The missing link is awareness, commitment, and the willpower to resolve structural obstacles.

The European Commission concluded that at least 20% of the energy used in the EU is wasted, with sheer inefficiency being the primary cause. The Commission determined that the EU could save an equal amount of energy by 2020 through cost-effective efficiency and conservation measures.[78]

When fulfilling our obligation to cut energy consumption, we have a special moral duty to eliminate energy use that serves no useful purpose such as the energy required for luxury goods such as second homes and gas-guzzling sport utility vehicles (SUVs). Next in line would be the elimination of energy use for amusements and trivial activities such as riding all-terrain vehicles (ATVs) for sport. These uses merely waste energy and generate needless emissions. No matter where we start, the point is that each of us, and each organization, has a moral responsibility to immediately eliminate all unnecessary energy consumption.[79]

Cuts in energy use alone, however, will not be sufficient to bring emissions down to safe levels. We must also significantly reduce material consumption because many products have huge energy value-chains. Fossil-fuel-based energy is required to extract minerals, metals, fiber, and other substances and transport them to processing facilities. Energy is then required to process and deliver the materials to manufacturing plants, where more energy is used to turn the raw materials into products and then package and deliver them to customers. Wholesalers and retailers use energy to store, market, and sell the products. "Users" – meaning us – then consume energy to operate many of the products. Energy is also required to transport broken and worn-out products to landfills and other waste disposal facilities, where more energy is used to manage the sites and ameliorate their environmental impacts. At each step greenhouse gas emissions are generated. To slash emissions we must therefore cut our material consumption.

Simple math is another reason material and energy consumption must be reduced. As I said earlier, the 7 billion-plus people living on the planet today are already consuming over 140% of the planet's resources. Billions more aspire to rise out of poverty and live a better life. If just a fraction of them are successful – and they have every right to be so – an even greater amount of the Earth's resources will be required. Moreover, government agencies are expecting global population to rise from to over 8 billion people by 2030 and to more than 9 billion by 2050.[80]

I am not at all convinced that the global population will ever reach 8 or 9 billion for the simple reason that climate disruption-induced droughts, heat waves, floods, and sea-level rise are likely to trigger large-scale famines and mass migrations that will constrain population. But, even if population does not grow as projected, our consumption must be radically reduced to allow those living in poverty today, and whatever number of humans that will join us in coming decades, to live decent lives without completely destroying the biosphere and pushing the climate into a permanent state of instability.

The moral obligation to rise above economic self-interest

The cost factor mentioned in the McKinsey report[81] leads to another important implication of our moral obligation to "do no harm." No individual, organization, or nation can look solely to their own economic self-interest when determining their response to climate disruption, the biodiversity crisis, or any other of today's emergencies. This moral obligation is essential because if programs and policies to address these problems are to gain sufficient public support, people must believe they will be fairly applied.

Wealthy nations such as the U.S., UK, and others in Europe have, over the past century, contributed the most to climate disruption. The U.S. is the world's largest total contributor, generating about 30% of the total energy-related carbon dioxide emissions that are destabilizing the climate. Collectively, the nations that compose the European Union produce the second largest cumulative amount of carbon dioxide. On an annual basis, the U.S. continues to produce far more emissions that any nation other than China.

If those of us living in Western nations are the worst offenders, then fair solutions must affect us the most. Yet, after attending a number of UN climate summits, it became evident to me that the U.S. has been one of the most strident opponents of meaningful emissions reductions. The U.S. is the only industrial country that chose not to sign the Kyoto Protocol. It has also worked actively behind the scenes to block any type of new binding international emissions reduction agreement.

The chief argument used by the U.S. to oppose serious efforts to address climate disruption is that the costs of emission reductions are too high. In other words, U.S. politicians and corporate leaders have said it will be too expensive to curtail practices that are injuring and killing millions of people. This is morally reprehensible. If you lived in regions of the world hardest hit by climate disruption, how would you respond to hearing someone say it will cost the U.S. too much to stop hurting you?

Policies that limit the ability of the poor to generate emissions while allowing those of us in wealthy nations to continue business-as-usual are morally unjust. Each American, each household, and every organization has a moral obligation to ignore the opposition of their government and rapidly reduce their use of materials, energy, and greenhouse gas emissions.

The moral obligation to place the climate and biosphere above human economic needs and rights

The solution to the global economic downturn that began in 2007 promoted by most economists and politicians was to get the economy growing again. But more growth using our current economic model will only worsen the climate and biodiversity crises. For example, the U.S. Congress allocated about $60 billion of the reported $787 billion included in the American Recovery and Reinvestment Act of 2009 – also called the Stimulus Bill – for highway improvements and other transportation and infrastructure projects, primarily to create jobs.[82] But the massive amount of concrete that was poured to repair roads and build other infrastructure undoubtedly added to the climate crisis because concrete is a very greenhouse-gas-intensive product. We once again put economic needs above the needs of the climate and natural environment. Although this type of job creation seemed imperative in the short term, in the long term it further degraded the basis of life upon which all jobs and economic well-being depend.

It is a rare occurrence when humans decide that protection of the natural environment is a higher priority than manipulating it for human use. When environmental protections occur it is usually to establish minimum standards that kick in only after air, water, or other environmental resources have been degraded to a low level, or to prevent the last remaining species from going extinct.[83] But the suffering and death resulting from climate disruption and the breakdown of the biosphere are deeply moral issues that demand a very different approach. Protection of the natural environment must now take priority over all economic activities that might degrade it. Each of us personally, and society as a whole, must constrain economic activities that impact the climate and biosphere in order to obtain the long-term benefit of a livable planet for our children and all future generations.

The moral obligation to rescue the innocent and protect the most vulnerable

The moral duty not to abuse others that is part and parcel of our moral obligation to "do no harm" means we have a special responsibility to assist the most vulnerable people and communities to withstand and bounce back from the impacts of climate disruption, ecological breakdown, and their associated social and economic ills. Even though climate disruption affects everyone, the Earth is warming faster near the equator and the poles. People living in less developed, low-latitude, hotter regions of the world, as well as in cold locations such as the Arctic, are thus initially the most affected by climate disruption. Yet they have contributed very little to the problem and have no say in what Western nations do.

By contrast, the U.S., European nations, and other developed countries have generated the largest amount of carbon dioxide emissions but appear, at least in the near term, to be least impacted by climate disruption.

A similar pattern holds true within the U.S. and Europe where low-income communities, working-class neighborhoods, communities of color, and children have contributed the least to climate disruption but have the fewest resources to protect themselves, and the least capacity to recover from impacts.

This is morally unjust. In order to enrich ourselves, wealthier people and nations are stealing from the poor and most vulnerable and abusing the defenseless. None of us living in the West can deny our responsibility for these problems. There are no innocent bystanders when it comes to climate disruption and ecosystem degradation. There is nothing innocent about idly standing by and doing nothing when you have the capacity in both small and large ways to avert or minimize the suffering and death caused by today's crises. Doing nothing is a gross violation of our moral duty to rescue and protect the most vulnerable.

Every one of us, and every organization, has a moral obligation to reduce our contribution to the problems. We also have a responsibility to urge others to reduce their contribution.

We must, in addition, demand that our governments provide financial resources and technologies necessary to allow the poor and most vulnerable within our nations, and in less developed countries across the world, to prepare for and adapt to the ecological, economic, and social consequences of climate disruption. And we have a moral obligation to help them grow their economies with as few emissions as possible by sharing the clean energy and production technologies that are emerging in the West.

The moral imperative to reduce economic inequality

Despite the many promises made in the past, Western nations are not likely to provide significant levels of assistance to less developed regions until we stop abusing people within our *own* nations by perpetuating huge economic inequalities. The greatest inequality in wealth among Western nations exists in the U.S., and it is no coincidence that the U.S. has failed to round up the $30 billion in financial aid it promised at the 2009 Copenhagen international climate summit to help poor nations respond to climate change.[84] The huge disparity in wealth dampens the American public's support for giving aid to others.

More equal countries, in contrast, tend to pay a higher percentage of their national income to foreign aid. Some of these countries, such as Sweden and Norway, give four times the proportion of their national income to assist other countries compared to less equal nations such as the U.S. and UK. The inequalities in wealth that affect the way people treat each other within their own nations clearly influence their approach to international affairs.[85]

For decades economists and politicians have told us that the way to resolve poverty is through more economic growth. Everyone will eventually benefit if the economic pie continues to grow larger, so the mantra goes. The promise of future growth is used to placate the masses that live in the middle and lower end of the economic spectrum. Henry Wallich, former governor of the U.S. Federal Reserve, framed this argument well by stating, "Growth is a substitute for equality of income. So long as there is growth there is hope, and that makes large income differentials tolerable."[86]

If economic growth is no longer possible because we have reached the physical limits of the Earth, then this argument has lost its validity. People will not be able to rise out of poverty through increased economic growth. If we are to avoid violent social and political backlash that will follow when the poor of the world realize this, economic inequality must be reduced to allow them access to sufficient levels of wealth needed to live a decent life.

Complete economic equality is not likely to occur without dictatorial control. Nor is it even desirable. Each of us, and each of the organizations we participate in, should be rewarded for exemplary effort and skill. Full economic equality, especially if mandated by government, would be unfair to those who are most innovative, create new solutions, and work hard. As the former communist regime in the Soviet Union found, complete equality is not an effective way to organize economic systems. But the huge discrepancies in income and wealth that exist in Western societies today are just as harmful as mandated equality because they produce a raft of health and social problems.

The income difference between senior executives and line workers in many U.S. corporations today is 500:1. There is no credible justification for the claim that executives are 500 times more important to an organization than other workers. Somewhere around a 15:1 ratio of pay between executives and staff seems to be the maximum possible to be considered a fair and equitable distribution of income and wealth.[87]

Corporate CEOs will tell you that the great disparities in income and wealth are simply a function of the market. There is some truth to this. Companies often have to pay more to attract and retain top talent. But this is also a convenient justification for greed. The reality is that public policies, pushed through by the rich, play a central role in creating the great accumulation of wealth at the top. This makes inequality a deeply moral issue. We must make a moral choice to adopt policies that equalize these disparities.

To help the most vulnerable people withstand the tremendous strains they are facing with climate disruption and lost biodiversity we must reduce income inequalities within our *own* nations. To "do no harm" to others we must first "do no harm" to ourselves.

The moral obligation to practice restorative justice

Given the large historic and ongoing contribution of the U.S. and other Western nations to climate disruption, species extinction, and many other pressing dilemmas, each of us, and each of our organizations, now have an obligation to honor the principles of restorative justice. It's very likely that as the difficult times ahead unfold, people throughout the world will seek payback for the harm that has been done. Rather than merely trying to punish offenders, restorative justice focuses on making the victims of abuse whole again and, as much as possible, repairing the damage that has been done. Unless injury to people and the natural environment is repaired, additional insults are likely to push them over the limit into conditions that produce permanent harm.[88]

Throughout history, many forms of restorative justice have been practiced, including restitution. Restitution is not about punishment. It is an obligation for individuals or groups to give up their ill-gotten gains. It seeks to restore the value of whatever was illegally or unfairly taken. Giving financial and technical aid to the poorest and most vulnerable nations to prepare for and adapt to climate change and biodiversity loss should be seen as an example of this approach.

But restitution is not the only way to seek repair. The requirement of full disclosure, as practiced by South Africa's Truth and Reconciliation Commission, Victim Offender Reconciliation or Mediation Programs, and even Mothers Against Drunk Driving offer examples of other ways that justice can be reframed in future-oriented restorative terms. In each of these cases, the voice of the victim and their surviving families is all-important and the victims have direct contact with the offender in order to communicate the impact of their crime.[89]

Climate disruption and biodiversity extinction "victim's right's" programs similar to these examples might be needed to address the abuses of corporations, political think-tanks, lobbyists, government agencies, elected officials, and others that have blocked efforts to address climate disruption, destroyed the rainforests, and in other ways violated the moral principle to "do no harm." The victims – people living in poor nations, the most vulnerable within Western nations, as well as children whose future is diminished by these practices – would have a chance to stand face to face with offenders and tell their stories. In turn, the officials would be able to confess their sins directly to the victims and to the world at large, and apologize. If falsely accused, they would have the opportunity to explain why. This process will help clear the air and make it possible to move forward together in order to develop collaborative solutions.

Restorative justice programs should not eliminate criminal or civil challenges. Nor should they replace the requirements of restitution. They should instead complement the legal process and offer the possibility that justice can serve a restorative, not just a punitive role.

What do you stand for?

When deciding on whether to abide by the principles of moral justice, it's important to ask yourself a critical question: "What do I stand for?" To answer this question you must determine how you will treat other people. How do you want to live your life? How do you want to be remembered? As you lie on your deathbed looking back on your time on Earth, what will you think about? Will you consider how much more "stuff" you could have acquired and how dominant you were? Or, will you remember the love you received and the caring you gave others? How do you want your gravestone inscribed? "She took everything she could for herself and caused others great harm," or "He traveled lightly and brought peace and happiness to others." The moral principles you adopt to guide your thinking and behavior determine what you stand for and what your legacy will be.

This truth applies to organizations as well. It is easy for private, public, and non-profit organizations to lose their way unless they continually question why it matters that they exist. Generating sufficient profit and making a decent income are important, but if your organization does not stand for anything beyond making money then it has very little inherent value to society. After all, many other organizations can sell the same products or do the same thing as yours. Making money is not a reason to exist – it is the outcome of achieving a higher purpose.

Given the difficult period of rapid, chaotic change we have entered, every organization that wants to survive in the future will need to choose a purpose that helps people navigate the turbulent waters ahead and emerge solidly grounded in sustainable thinking and action. The moral principles your organization adopts will determine its ability to achieve that purpose. Financial well-being will be just one of the outcomes.

Abiding by the principles of moral justice can enhance the economy

It should be no surprise that abiding by the principles of moral justice opens the door to tremendous economic opportunity. Dramatic cuts in material and energy consumption, for example, offer the prospect of significant cost savings. Such cuts will reduce pressure on energy prices, strengthen the economy of communities, and improve the bottom line of businesses. Reduced material and energy use will protect the poor and those on fixed incomes, and diminish air pollutants, leading to better public health.

Further, a just and equitable transition to a zero-carbon economy will, over time, generate millions of good jobs in zero-carbon industries. This is important because we have a moral responsibility to be as concerned with the type of work humans do as we are with the number of jobs created. We do not want jobs that degrade the environment, harm other people, or concentrate wealth at the top of society. The jobs of the future must help restore the planet's social and ecological systems and reestablish a decent level of economic equality. Jobs producing, selling, repairing, and recycling zero-carbon goods and providing services offer the type of work society needs if it is to successfully address the challenges that lie ahead.

Greater economic equality will also increase the innovation needed to solve the climate, biodiversity, and economic crises. Despite the belief held by many, the U.S. and UK are not the most entrepreneurial nations in the world. At least as defined by the number of patents issue per capita, nations that are more equal are much more innovative. This may be due to the fact that in more unequal nations people at the lower levels cannot obtain the financial resources needed to scale up an idea, or that few of these would-be entrepreneurs believe their innovations will help them achieve higher economic status. No matter what the reason, the data shows that innovation is greatest in nations that are more economically equal. Reducing economic inequities can therefore help spur people to create new solutions to today's problems.[90]

The truth is that the way out of our economic troubles is the same as the path that can resolve today's environmental crisis – a moral commitment to "do no harm" by creating greater equality that helps stimulate the innovation needed to dramatically reduce consumption, combined with increased investments in zero-carbon technologies and renewable energy that create good jobs. The right moral choice is also the right choice for business, workers, families, communities, and governments worldwide, as well as for the climate and biosphere.

Of course, it will take at least a decade of hard work under trying circumstances for these rewards to come to fruition. And, if we fail to quickly alter our thinking and behavior and marshal our resources, none of these benefits will materialize.

Moral justice brings tangible personal benefits

Morally just behavior benefits each of us personally as well. Your ability to form close personal relationships, for instance, is enhanced when people trust that you will treat them fairly. Acting morally will also be a key determinant in the success of your career.

More importantly, abiding by a clear set of high moral standards is a key to your sense of happiness and well-being. A strong orientation toward selfish "Me" behavior, including high consumption patterns, produces a variety of psychological and physical health problems. For instance, studies from many different nations, involving both males and females, from pre-schoolers to the elderly, show that placing a high value on the acquisition of financial wealth and material goods, regardless of income levels, is associated with higher levels of anxiety, depression, and reduced life satisfaction. Individuals that consume a great deal are more likely to be insecure, engage in antisocial behavior, have personality disorders, and experience difficulties in intimate relationships.[91]

Furthermore, the lack of a moral commitment to low consumption reinforces feelings of personal insecurity. Whatever positive feeling we get from buying more "stuff" is generally short-lived, and we must then consume more "stuff" to get more positive feelings. This creates an acquisition treadmill, characterized by unhappiness and insecurity which stimulates more acquisition and subsequent insecurities. In the process, we neglect the social relationships that contribute to our sense of personal well-being. We also tend to become less empathetic and have a difficult time experiencing intimacy. This affects the people around us, including our children.[92]

In choosing to live a moral and just life you are making the ultimate choice about the type of person you want to be. You are shaping your personal identity. Your sense of self-worth, integrity, and honor are all very much determined by your capacity to live by a set of high moral standards.

Moral justice is a key to organizational success

Organizations also benefit from abiding by the principles of moral justice. Walker Information, a global stakeholder research firm, examined 13 academic studies of empirical evidence of the business outcomes of ethical corporate behavior.[93] They found that ethical behavior improves employee relations and leads to higher employee retention as well we better morale, loyalty, motivation, and productivity.

The study concluded that a firm's ethical stance leads to greater customer loyalty and a stronger brand image. Further, a commitment to ethical behavior was found to enhance the overall performance of the business, including improved competitive advantage, higher financial returns, and better reputation. These are factors that help to sustain an organization over the long term. Acting in a morally just manner is thus a key to organizational success.

Your moral stance will help you navigate through challenging times

Take a moment to reflect on the moral principles you currently use to guide your life. This might not be an easy task because we frequently live our lives on autopilot and fail to consider this question. Have you consciously chosen a clear set of moral precepts? If so, are you satisfied with what they signify about how you live your life? If you are content, take joy in the helpful things you have done. It is important to constantly acknowledge your moral commitments and the benefits they provide to you and others.

After some introspection, if you cannot describe the moral axioms that shape your interactions with other people and the natural environment, or you are dissatisfied with your current stance, put down in writing the principles you choose to live by from this point forward.

The moral principles you and your organization decide to live by will shape your response to the turbulent period of history we have entered. If you commit to practicing moral justice and make the shift from "Me" to "We," you can make the tough choices required to help society transition to true sustainability.

After you personally make this commitment, you can help the organizations you are engaged with make a similar change. The moral principles they adopt will determine their response to the climate and biodiversity crises and the economic and social turmoil they trigger.

As more people and more organizations practice moral justice, the shift from "Me" to "We" will accelerate and a powerful force will grow that leads us ever closer to true sustainability.

5
The fourth commitment
Acknowledge your trustee obligations and take responsibility for the continuation of all life

Examine, for a moment, the picture of the Earth taken by the Apollo 17 astronauts in 1972.[94] Called the "Blue Marble," this is the first and most complete picture humanity had ever seen of our planet – our home – as a whole.

The picture graphically shows there are no discharge pipes allowing us to dump our toxic substances, solid waste, and greenhouse gases into outer space. Everything we humans make – toxic and otherwise – accumulates somewhere in the land, waters, or atmosphere of our planet. And, as you can see, there are no intake pipelines that allow us to import additional resources from other planets. When we deplete non-renewable resources they will vanish forever. When we push the Earth's climate and ecological systems beyond their limits, they are likely to flip into permanently degraded and, from a human perspective, unwanted conditions.

The cumulative effects of human activities on the Earth – especially those of the past 50–100 years – have led a number of scientists to proclaim that we have entered a new geological era called the "Anthropocene." This term refers to the fact that, for the first time, humankind's influence on the environment is so overwhelming that our activities, rather than natural processes, will now determine the fate of the Earth.[95]

It is a universal moral principle that the more power one has over another, the greater is the duty to use that power benevolently. If human behaviors now determine the fate of the planet, individually and collectively, we have a responsibility to do what is necessary to sustain it. This is the **Law of Trusteeship**. This natural law of sustainability says that no one living today actually owns anything. We are merely trustees with a responsibility to administer the planet's assets to ensure that they are sustained in a healthy condition into perpetuity.

The trusteeship principle is as old as time. It describes the personal thinking, actions, and societal rules and regulations required to maintain and rebuild the social and ecological systems we all depend on for life. It is thus a centerpiece of the shift from "Me" to "We."

Acknowledging that we are trustees of all there is in the world is a difficult task for most people and most organizations. Our belief in extreme individualism, derived from the mistaken idea that we exist independently from all other organisms and processes on Earth, leads us to think that we have no responsibilities for anything beyond our organizations, our families, and ourselves. This belief is erroneous. **The fourth commitment you and the organizations you are involved with must make to realize the shift from "Me" to "We" that is essential to resolving today's many crises, is to acknowledge your trustee obligations and take responsibility for the continuation of all life.**

While the commitment to abide by the moral precept to "do no harm" seeks to control the selfish and aggressive aspects of our nature, the commitment to acknowledge your trustee obligations and take responsibility for the continuation of all life emphasizes our selfless, cooperative, and caring instincts. It thus operationalizes the second of humanity's most deeply held universal moral principles, which is to "do good." Each of us has an inherent drive toward health. Well-being comes about when the different aspects of our personalities are integrated.[96] Our innate drive to "do good" helps to bring about this integration. The Golden Rule succinctly describes this commitment: "Treat others as you would like them to treat you."

What does the principle of trusteeship actually mean? One way to understand it is to think of the Earth as a "living trust." In a legal sense, a living trust is the transfer of assets – which can include tangible resources such as land or financial capital, as well as intangible assets such as goodwill – into a trust that exists while you are still alive. The person or group that establishes the living trust delegates the responsibility for administering it to a "trustee," which can be an individual, organization, or group. Those who ultimately receive the yield or benefits provided by the living trust are the beneficiaries.

Our little Blue Marble is a living organism and thus is the ultimate living trust. We are all trustees of this perpetual living trust. We are all responsible for it. We are also all beneficiaries, as are our children, grandchildren, and all future generations.

One of the core requirements of a trustee of a living trust is that they clearly understand their responsibilities. As defined by numerous trust documents, the most important include: the duty of loyalty; the duty of prudence; the duty to monitor; and the duty to disclose.[97]

The 'duty of loyalty'

The "duty of loyalty" means that the trustees of the living trust must always act solely in the best interests of, and for the exclusive purposes of, providing benefits to the beneficiaries. This has long been considered the most fundamental duty of a trustee. The physical and intangible "assets" of the trust cannot be appropriated for the use and benefits of a limited number of trustees. A trustee must also avoid conflicts of interests by not selling to, purchasing from, or otherwise dealing with him- or herself.

Although a trustee cannot "profit" from his or her role, they can be reasonably compensated for the work managing the living trust.

The standard of behavior expected of a trustee is stricter than the practices of today's marketplace. Under the "duty of loyalty" trustees are expected to uncompromisingly act in the best interests of the trust, even if market forces pressure them to do otherwise. Claims by trustees that they acted "in good faith" are not acceptable excuses for violating this duty. They must do what is necessary, not merely do their best.

The "duty of impartiality" is an integral part of the "duty of loyalty." Trustees must be "super-fair." They are not permitted to show favoritism toward any single member or group of beneficiaries.

As part of their "duty of loyalty," a trustee is obligated not to delegate to others functions that they can perform themselves.

Responsibilities that a trustee cannot execute, which should be very few, can be delegated to an agent. When delegation occurs, however, the trustees have a personal duty to choose qualified agents that do not have a conflict of interest, and to closely supervise those agents just as any prudent person would.

When we compare much of our behavior to these duties it becomes abundantly clear that many of us, and many of our organizations and governments, consistently violate our "duty of loyalty."

The duty not to appropriate trust assets for private gain

The Earth's resources such as minerals, forests, fresh water, and the generic structures of plants and animals, as well as public assets such as the Internet, the airwaves, and government-funded research are increasingly being taken over and, in some cases, even patented by private interests. The appropriation of these assets is degrading the health of the natural environment, undermining democratic processes, and shifting ownership and control of the living trust that is the Earth from the beneficiaries – meaning each of us and all future generations – to a few private interests.

Rather than protecting the assets of the living trust, our governments are in many cases actively violating their "duty of loyalty" by giving them away for free, selling them at low discounts, or marketizing assets that should never be bought or sold in the first place.[98]

Further, as discussed, those of us who live in rich nations are using substantially more natural resources than those in poor counties. Many of those resources are taken from poor regions of the world at a low price while leaving behind broken communities and degraded ecosystems. We have also appropriated much more than our fair share of the "atmospheric space" available for greenhouse gas emissions.

These are direct violations of our "duty to loyalty" which requires us to prevent the assets of the living trust that is the Earth from being used for private gain by a limited number of trustees or beneficiaries.

The duty to an equitable distribution of compensation

Although trustees cannot "profit" from their role, they can be compensated for their effort. When applied to the Earth as a living trust, this means that each of us, and each of our organizations, can retain a portion of the proceeds derived from our work on the planet. However, each individual's earnings must not be greatly out of proportion to others, and the majority of the proceeds must be reinvested in ways that help sustain and regenerate the assets of the living trust. This is certainly not occurring today.

The most recent data shows that in 2007 the top 1% of U.S. earners received 23% of the nation's total income. This is almost triple the 8% share they held in 1980. The top 1% also owned over 34% of all privately held wealth. The top 20% of the populace owned 85% of the wealth while the remaining 80% of the people owned just 15%.[99]

In the UK, the richest 10% of the population are more than 100 times wealthier than the poorest 10%. When the top 1% of the highest-paid workers, including bankers and chief executives, are added to the equation, the gaps in wealth get even worse.[100]

Although the U.S. and UK have the largest inequality in incomes and wealth, similar patterns show up in many other Western nations.

Even more startling gaps exist between rich and poor nations. The U.S., with less than 5% of the world's population, holds about $50 trillion in wealth, or 25% of total global wealth. Europe, with about 11% of the world's population, as a region owns about 32% of total wealth.[101]

Another way to view this situation is that about 3 billion people, or more than two-thirds of the global adult population, have per capita wealth below $10,000 a year. Another billion adults, or about 24% of the world adult population, have per capita wealth ranging from $10,000 to $100,000 a year. About 24 million individuals, or less than 1% of the global adult population, own more than a third of total global household wealth.[102]

As discussed in the previous chapter, complete economic equality is not likely to occur (without dictatorial mandates), nor is it even desirable. But the huge inequality in wealth shows that many of us, and many of our organizations, are violating their "duty of loyalty" by appropriating for themselves far more than their fair share of the proceeds from the living trust that is the Earth.

The duty to become aware and accept our responsibilities

The obligation to refrain from delegating our duties as trustees to others, except in the rare cases where we do not have the needed skills, means no individual, and no organization, can abdicate their responsibility to protect and enhance the living trust that is the Earth. No individual can claim to be unaware of their responsibilities. Businesses cannot claim their only duty is to make money or increase shareholder value and that it is government's job to care for the living trust's social and ecological systems. As trustees, we all have a responsibility to manage the living trust to preserve the well-being of its assets for the common good of all current and future beneficiaries.

Equally as important is the fact that no government can abandon its "duty of loyalty." In most Western nations the responsibility for administering "public goods" – things no single person or organization can provide or manage on their own but which everyone uses and relies on such as the air, water, and oceans – has historically been delegated to government. The climate and biosphere are public goods, not private assets. Government must act in the public interest and sustain them for all current and future beneficiaries.

Government oversight is also required to guide the market. Our belief in separation and extreme individualism leads many people to conclude that markets are god-like mechanisms that exist independently from the social and ecological systems in which they are all embedded. This is nonsense. Markets are merely ways of organizing social relationships to produce and exchange goods and services.

Markets have generated considerable good, and also a great deal of harm over the past decades. These outcomes have little to do with markets themselves. They are the results of the beliefs and values people hold that lead them to design the market in certain ways. If enough people make the shift from "Me" to "We," the goals, rules, practices – and thus the outcomes – of the market will change. As with so many other issues today, dysfunctional markets are the outcome of flawed human thinking and design, not something inherently wrong with markets themselves.

Government plays an essential role in shaping how markets function by establishing and enforcing laws and regulations. In fact, the market as we know it today would not exist without government. Through its legislative, regulatory, and judicial systems government provides essential functions such as ensuring property rights, enforcing contracts, acting as a referee, ensuring product quality and safety, maintaining fair competition, and imposing penalties for foul play. It also provides public and quasi-public goods that are essential to the market but which the market will not supply, or at least not supply at sufficient levels, such as defense, security, police protection, physical infrastructure, relief to the poor and unemployed, education, health care, and retirement benefits. Indeed, laws, regulations, and enforcement mechanisms are the foundation of modern markets.

Because we have entrusted government with the responsibility for overseeing many aspects of the living trust that is the Earth, it has a responsibility to set limits, enact laws, and enforce regulations that protect its assets for the benefit of all current and future beneficiaries. True sustainability requires that we mutually agree to constrain our short-term desires for long-term payoffs. While many people can constrain their selfish and aggressive qualities by voluntarily choosing to abide by deeply held moral precepts, rules and regulation by government are essential to curb the behavior of those who cannot control themselves. Currently, however, few governments are adequately meeting their responsibilities.

Large corporations today hold as much or even more influence than governments over the living trust that is the Earth. Many of them have failed to honor their "duty of loyalty" by using methods and producing products and services that continually degrade, rather than maintain, the planet's social and ecological systems.

The duty to treat all beneficiaries fairly

The duty to impartiality that is a central element of the "duty of loyalty" requires that all of the beneficiaries of the living trust be dealt with fairly. The huge inequalities in income and wealth that exist today within Western nations, and between them and poor countries, violate this duty. Inequality also undermines a sense of fairness and breeds cynicism that makes it difficult, if not impossible, for people to band together and solve common problems such as economic collapse and climate disruption.

Developed nations that are more economically equal, such as the northern European nations of Sweden, Denmark, and Norway, as well as Japan, have achieved high standards of living (and some indications indicate higher) with far fewer health and social problems compared to those with large inequalities such as the U.S. and UK. They also have a greater commitment to environmental protection as demonstrated by higher recycling rates, lower per capita greenhouse gas emissions, and give more per capita in foreign aid to poor nations to prepare for, and adapt to, climate disruption.[103]

These indicators show that when people are treated fairly, society as a whole ends up better off.

It is not just the current populace that is being treated unfairly. We are also not treating future beneficiaries – our children and all future generations – equitably. If our hunter–gatherer ancestors had damaged the natural environment in the same way and scale as we are doing today, few of us would even be here! The difference between our Stone Age ancestors and us is that we are acting with more than adequate knowledge of the consequences and yet we continue to do so for profit, power, and privilege. Only by honoring the "duty of impartiality" that is central to our "duty of loyalty" can we ensure that future generations have the same opportunities as we do.

The 'duty of prudence'

Let us now turn our focus to the "duty of prudence." This duty means that a trustee of the living trust that is the Earth must discharge their duties with the same care, skill, prudence, and diligence that any prudent person would use if they were managing other valued assets under their control. They must utilize the most current data, use state-of-the-art processes and technologies, and continually scan the horizon for future risks and opportunities. Trustees are responsible for damages if they use lesser skills or capacities.

Trustees can invest portions of the trust's assets to advantage the beneficiaries. However, investments must be diversified to minimize the risk of loss, and risky investments must be avoided. Speculation is explicitly prohibited because of the potential loss for beneficiaries.

The "duty of prudence" also means that trustees must acquire the knowledge and skills needed to effectively discharge their responsibilities as a trustee. This means that the trustees must take reasonable steps to educate themselves about how their living trust works, what their responsibilities are, and how to capably perform them.

The duty to abandon the idea of continuous economic growth

One of the most important implications of the duty to diversify investments and avoid risky activities is the requirement for those of us living in Western nations to abandon the belief that economic growth is the solution to all of our problems. The truth is that more economic growth in wealthy nations will only hasten the collapse of many of the core systems of the living trust that is the Earth. Rather than continually pushing for additional growth, Western nations must find ways to improve quality of life through much greater diversification of energy and material resources, and by using and reusing existing capital with significantly less material consumption, energy use, greenhouse gas emissions, and solid waste.

Most of the important social benefits of continual economic growth came to an end in Western nations in the 1970s: a fact that few people will admit. Research has consistently found that up to a certain level, economic growth is important. Material gain allows people at the lowest economic strata to overcome physical, emotional, and psychological problems associated with economic deprivation. For individuals in the middle classes and above, however, the links between additional money, health, and happiness are almost non-existent.[104]

Despite steady economic growth, as measured by GDP and other indicators over the past 30 years, health and social problems have actually increased, not decreased, especially in the U.S. and UK, but also in other rich countries. As mentioned, one of the reasons for this is that much of the growth has been siphoned off by 10% or less of the populace creating a small class of the super-rich, while the rest of us have seen our real incomes and wealth stagnate or decline. Without policies that significantly reduce economic equality, more growth will create an even wealthier upper class with commensurate economic and political power, leaving the rest of us in worse shape than before.

In addition, more growth requires more consumption of energy and raw materials, which will generate more greenhouse gases, and further destabilize the climate.

Just as importantly, trying to grow the economy without significant changes in economic equality will only put added pressure on people in the middle and lower economic classes to consume more in order to avoid losing ground or feeling inferior to those in the upper levels. Many will live beyond their means, eat into their meager savings, and go into debt simply to keep up. This is one of the dynamics that contributed to the 2008 global economic collapse.

The duty to redesign our production systems

In order to find new ways to meet human needs without more economic growth, our systems of production must be fundamentally redesigned. The production model of Western nations today can be considered a "take it, make it, and waste it" approach. We extract materials from the face of the Earth, convert them into products for human use, and emit massive amounts of solid, liquid, and gaseous wastes, including greenhouse gases, with little thought of the consequences for the Earth's social or ecological systems. We believe that increased efficiency and after-the-fact remediation will address any side-effects generated throughout this process. However, like so many of our current beliefs, this is just wishful thinking. The extent of the damage produced by our linear "take–make–waste" production model overwhelms all attempts to ameliorate the consequences after the fact.

The alternative to the linear approach is a "closed-loop" or "cradle-to-cradle" production system. In this model, all technical materials used in industrial or commercial processes are continually recirculated back into the economy for additional uses. This allows materials to be used over and over again without being "downcycled" into lesser products that ultimately become waste. Toxic substances must be eliminated to achieve this goal. After use, all biological or organic materials are reintroduced into nature where they can decompose and serve as nutrients for new growth. To prevent harm to ecosystems, toxic substances must be eliminated from biological materials as well.[105]

Many examples of closed-loop systems are emerging across the globe. They need to be scaled up. New policies, new technologies, new practices, and new infrastructure are needed to accomplish this. Above all, scaling-up of closed-loop systems will require a change of perspective from focusing only on "Me" to prioritizing the broader "We."

The duty to use resources sustainably

If we give up the notion that more economic growth is possible, we must use natural resources at levels that allow them to naturally regenerate. We breach our "duty of prudence" every time we knowingly use natural resources faster than they can be replenished or generate pollution and greenhouse gas emissions faster than the Earth can naturally break down and sequester them.

Despite ample scientific knowledge of current conditions and the technical capacity to manage for sustained harvest, for example, roughly half of the forests that once covered the Earth are gone, and each year about another 39 million acres disappear. Marine fisheries are being overfished and water resources are being depleted at alarming rates. Nutrients in agricultural soils are being exhausted and water resources are being degraded far faster than they can be naturally restored.

The scientific evidence that we are in dangerous territory with climate change has been available for at least 20 years. Yet we have ignored this data and allowed emissions to continue to grow.

We are clearly not using our best knowledge and skills to manage the living trust's natural systems. Few of us would manage our own cherished assets such as personal savings or private homes this recklessly.

The duty to follow the precautionary principle

The ban on speculation that is part and parcel of the "duty of prudence" means that each of us, and each organization, has a duty to honor the "precautionary principle." This principle, which emerged from the Rio Earth Summit in 1992 and was endorsed by most of the nations of the world, including the U.S., says that when an action or policy has potential risks to the public or the natural environment, precautionary measures should be taken, even if some of the cause-and-effect relationships are not completely established by science. The burden of proof that an activity is *not* harmful must fall on the proponent of the action or policy. It is not the public's responsibility to prove the existence of harmful outcomes before a product or activity can be banned. Proponents must prove that an action is benign through the analysis of independent experts, not people paid by the industry. We cannot speculate with the assets of the living trust that is the Earth.

The duty to prepare for and adapt to climate disruption

No matter how rapidly greenhouse gas emissions are reduced, global temperatures seem certain to rise to dangerous levels. Extreme drought, windstorms, heat waves and other events will become more frequent and sea levels will rise. Surprise events should be allowed for as well. The "duty of prudence" requires that every trustee, and each of the current beneficiaries of the living trust that is the Earth, aggressively build their capacity to withstand and adapt to these impacts. As ironic as this sounds, of special importance is the need to rapidly build resiliency in regions of the world that will be *least* affected by climate disruption because they will become safe havens and refuges for people and biota worldwide.

Three core principles can help you and your organization prepare for climate disruption and other stresses.[106]

The first principle is to **build diversity and redundancy**. Just as a diversified suite of financial investments is more likely to withstand fluctuations in the stock market, diversified ecological and human systems are better equipped to withstand and adapt to stresses caused by climate disruption. Within limits, many organisms are naturally endowed with the behavioral, developmental, and genetic traits needed to adjust to major disturbances such as droughts, fires, and flood events. In some cases, for example, they might disperse to other regions and in other cases they might become dormant. The protection and restoration of a wide range of biotic diversity along with their habitats is thus essential to ensure that organisms with different response types survive. It is also important because of the need to maintain the ecological systems that are an essential element of the Earth's capacity to self-regulate.

Diversity and redundancy are also essential within organizations. In resilient organizations, for instance, more than one person is authorized to make decisions, which allows operations to continue even when the top executive is absent. They also have multiple ways to communicate and to continuously provide essential goods and services.

Resilient communities have a diverse and redundant array of businesses and job types. They have backup systems to ensure a steady supply of energy, and multiple ways to distribute essential goods and services, communicate, and transport people.

The less diversity and redundancy that exists within ecological and social systems the more vulnerable they are to stresses of all types, including those triggered by climate disruption.

The second principle is to **manage for disturbance and change**. Many of the problems we face today are the result of past efforts to control change. Dams were built, for example, to ensure ample supplies of water in droughts and to control floods. Industrial agriculture came to dominate in part because steady supplies of large quantities of food could be produced at low prices even when crops failed in certain regions.

Despite the good intentions, over the long haul these actions have reduced ecological and social resiliency. Soil fertility in the floodplain is depleted when a stream is never allowed to flood. Insects and disease can easily destroy crops grown in industrial monocultures.

The same dynamic occurs in social systems. Businesses that are not allowed to fail reduce the innovation and dynamism of the economy. Management programs established to address a specific problem often remain in place long after the original need has faded away, which siphons away resources needed for new initiatives and undermines organizational effectiveness.

Resilient ecological and social systems allow for some level of natural disturbances. Moderate flooding, for example, increases gravel and woody debris in a stream, which in turn helps limit the effects of a major flood while enriching the soils. Allowing outdated businesses to fail rather than propping them up with subsidies allows products and services to enter the market that are better suited for changing conditions.

The third principle is to **promote modularity**. This relates to the way and extent to which the key variables of a system are connected. The more tightly linked the components are, the more susceptible they become to shocks that rapidly move through the entire system, producing damaging effects at multiple scales. In contrast, the more loosely connected a system is the greater the likelihood that some of its parts can avoid serious harm when major disturbances occur.

The global financial meltdown that began in 2007 demonstrates the risk of over-connectedness in human systems. A problem that originated in the U.S. quickly spread across the globe because world financial systems had become deeply enmeshed. Don't try to tightly link everything. Instead, build resistance and resiliency within loosely connected, modular processes, structures, and nodes.

These three principles can help each household, organization, and community prepare for and adapt to the strains generated by climate disruption and other challenges that will unfold in the coming decades. The "duty of prudence" requires that we build resiliency and prepare for the impacts before they become too severe. Particular emphasis should be put on creating climate safe havens wherever possible, with resiliency becoming the central goal of all local ecological, social, and economic systems.

The duty to become educated in sustainable thinking and acting

Finally, the responsibility of all trustees to acquire the knowledge and skills needed to effectively manage the living trust that is the Earth means that each individual must become reasonably educated about how to live sustainably. Ignorance, rather than maliciousness or greed, is often the reason some people think and act unsustainably. Before you are allowed to drive a vehicle you are required to learn the rules of the road and pass a driving test. Similarly, all trustees of the living trust – meaning all of us – should be required to learn the rules of the road involved with true sustainable thinking and acting.

This type of learning must take place in early childhood education all the way up to adult continuing education. As I have stressed throughout this book, the most important focus of the educational process must be to help people shift their perspectives from "Me" to "We" and learn how to think and act sustainably.

The 'duty to monitor' and the 'duty to disclose'

The "duty to monitor" and the "duty to disclose" are closely linked. The former requires that trustees continually evaluate the conditions and "performance" of the living trust to ensure that it can continue to provide for future beneficiaries. The latter means that trustees have an obligation to honestly disclose to all beneficiaries any negative conditions that may exist. Transparency is a core element of this duty.

To fulfill these duties, each individual, household, and organization must regularly analyze their ecological and social footprints. Do you and your organization know how much raw material and energy you consume each year, and what the social, economic, and environmental consequences might be from this use? These calculations must become standard practice and the results must be made public. Perhaps once a year local newspapers should publish the footprints of each resident and organization, just as many of them publish articles on current income levels and the rate of economic growth.

As noted, the responsibility for administering many of the living trust's assets has historically been delegated to government.

We expect our governments to continually monitor the living trust that is the Earth on a regular basis and give us honest, straightforward assessments of conditions and trends. Our governments must also proactively investigate potential risks and identify the perpetrators of damage. When our government fails to perform these duties, they violate their "duty to monitor" and "duty to disclose."

The trustee role of business

Just as most individuals envision themselves as separate entities, many businesses today largely see themselves as distinct from society and the natural environment. CEOs often proclaim that a business has one purpose only – to maximize profit for the owners or, if it is a public corporation, to maximize shareholder value. All other goals are secondary, or the responsibility of others. The principle of trusteeship offers the business community an alternative perspective to this erroneous and harmful belief.

The trusteeship model views a business as being the temporary trustee of everything it uses and does. Remember; whether it's a huge international corporation or a small family-owned firm, a business is merely a social system – a way of structuring human relationships to produce certain outcomes. It is a physical reality that each of the people involved with a business are here on Earth for just a short time. This means that no business actually "owns" anything. They are just temporary stewards of the assets they hold. The trustee model requires that each business administer that wealth to ensure the well-being of all of the current and future beneficiaries of the living trust.

This perspective helps executives and workers see that private gains are possible only with the help of many other people locally and abroad, as well as the use of public goods such as roads, educational systems, the climate, and the biosphere. Everything a business does must therefore benefit the social and ecological systems that make its success possible. Business practices must ensure the long-term health and well-being of the social and ecological systems of the living trust that is the Earth, or they cannot be considered economically viable.

To abide by the law of trusteeship a business must ask a key question: "Why do we exist?" As discussed in the previous chapter, if the company has no better answer than to make money or increase shareholder value, it has no inherent value to society. The people involved with the firm need to decide what their larger social purpose is, and what they stand for.

They must do so by first understanding the ecological and social context in which they exist. They must then seek to comprehend how the consequences of their actions, and the activities of others in society, might interact to affect that context. In other words, firms can honestly decide why they exist only after they grasp that humanity has hit the limits of the Earth's capacity to provide more resources and absorb more of our impacts without widespread damage and collapse. Then, and only then, can the question be honestly answered. The members of the firm will then need to decide if they will produce goods and services that serve the common good by helping society resolve issues such as climate disruption, ecosystem degradation, and economic inequity, or whether they will ignore these issues and simply pursue material gain and profit.

Businesses that choose the latter path are not likely to exist in the future because after people wake up to the precarious conditions of the planet they will demand a rapid end to such practices.

Businesses that choose to make the transition from "Me" to "We" must clarify what the results of a "We" orientation would look like for the organization. It must decide, for example, on the type of products or services it will offer, how they will be made, how the organization will operate internally, what its ecological and social footprints will be, and how people outside of the firm will be treated.

All executives, employees, owners, shareholders, and stakeholders then need to adopt beliefs, behaviors, practices, and policies that can produce those results.

In other words, trusteeship requires that the people involved with a business undergo a "second-order" change to sustainable thinking and practices. I will discuss how a business can make these changes in the next chapter.

A number of businesses have adopted principles of corporate social responsibility (CSR) to address these concerns. But in many organizations CSR is relegated to philanthropy and other nice but surface-level activities that have little affect on actual business practices. Rather than reorienting the organization to promote the common good, profit maximizing for the owners and shareholder value remain the true priorities. For CSR to have any real significance, it must be fully embraced by everyone and completely integrated into the organization. A culture of accountability for sustainable thinking and behavior is needed. This requires that each business realize that its duties to all of the beneficiaries of the living trust must always supersede its obligations to the firm's owners and shareholders.

The duty to demand allegiance to our trustee responsibilities

Perhaps the most important duty we each have as beneficiaries of the living trust that is the Earth is to stand firm and demand that everyone – including ourselves – abide by their trustee obligations.

On a personal level, before making a purchase always ask yourself: "Do I really need this item?" If it is not essential to your health and well-being, then don't buy it. When you do need goods, make it a habit to only buy recycled and used products or those certified by independent third parties as environmentally and socially sustainable. Don't use products, such as plastics, made from fossil fuels or those embedded with toxic materials or substances. Let local businesses know that you want products that are made of non-toxic, biodegradable materials that can be completely recycled. Insist that your local power utilities provide carbon-free renewable energy for use in your home and by the organizations and businesses in your community. Even better, produce the energy yourself using small-scale clean and renewable sources.

Consumer action alone, however, is not likely to change the way companies, or the market as a whole, operate. Public condemnation, legal challenges, political pressure, and other strategies will also be needed, especially for organizations that remain blinded by the belief in separation and extreme individualism and therefore behave egregiously (a number of coal, oil, gas, timber, and mining companies come to mind). Large U.S. corporations such as Arthur Andersen and Enron quickly vanished due to accounting and financial fraud. Any business that fails to honor its responsibilities to maintain and enhance the living trust that sustains us all should be forced to go the same route.

We must also demand that our governments follow through on their obligations as trustees of the living trust by enacting and enforcing effective and just laws and regulations. This requires much more than merely voting in elections. Extremely wealthy people and large corporations control politics in most Western nations today through the cash they supply to campaigns or political parties and the influence of lobbyists. They also have the ability to use the media and other venues to frame political debates in ways that persuade many citizens and officials that the top priority of government must be to protect their interests. Consequently, no matter whom we elect, our systems of governance always seem to keep churning in the same unsustainable direction.

Just as Americans once demanded "No taxation without representation," people worldwide must now demand "No legislation without representation." We must demand true representative democracy. The stranglehold that the "Me"-focused super-rich and large corporations have over our political system must be broken. We must elect governments that put real social and environmental sustainability at the forefront of their policies and work for all people and future generations. Just as species that improve the habitability of their environment flourish, and those that foul it become extinct, if it comes down to it we must refuse to cooperate with governments that fail to effectively perform their duties as trustees of the most important of all living trusts. As a last resort we may need to dismantle governments and establish truly democratic institutions.

Do you see yourself as a trustee of the living trust that is the Earth? To what extent do you strive to perform your duty of loyalty, duty of prudence, duty to monitor, and duty to disclose? How does your organization approach these issues?

Once you understand that what humans do today will determine the health and well-being of everything on the planet, you must acknowledge that we are trustees of the living trust that is the Earth. This understanding leads to only one conclusion: each of us must take responsibility for the continuation of all life on the planet.

6

The fifth commitment
Choose your own destiny

Consider this question: "What do you actually know for certain about the causes and solutions to our current economy, social, and environmental challenges?" Think hard. What are you personally 100% sure of? All sorts of ideas and facts are undoubtedly rumbling through your mind right now. Our brains are filled with a tremendous amount of data and notions that we have learned over the years. But what can you point to about today's circumstances that you know with absolute certainty?

Despite all we have learned in our lifetime we have not been able to prevent the breakdown of many of the core systems that sustain the planet and ourselves. Yet we continually strive to know more with the hope that the next piece of information will offer a path out of our predicament. Doesn't that seem strange?

So much of our knowing has failed to lead us to where we want to go because much of it is based on false assumptions and misperceptions. We don't actually know what we think we know. Understanding this is the most important step in the shift from

"Me" to "We" that is the centerpiece of sustainable thinking and action.

After we finally realize that most of what we know is not very helpful in resolving our current dilemmas, we begin to search for truths that are useful. The most valuable elements of any teaching are its fundamentals. The basics are easy to forget because our minds often become caught up in the minutiae and we miss the core elements. But the fundamentals are the most powerful keys to change.

The natural laws of sustainability and associated commitments described in this book are the fundamentals of the shift from "Me" to "We" embodied in sustainable thinking and action. In summary, these laws state that our survival and the survival of all other life forms on Earth is possible only because we are enmeshed within a complex web of interdependent climatic, ecological, and social systems. Given the deteriorating conditions of the planet today, almost every action we take affects those systems somewhere, at some point in time. Our response to these consequences will be shaped by the moral principles we adopt to guide our thinking, behavior, and policies. Because human actions now determine the fate of the Earth, like it or not, each of us is now a trustee with the responsibility to care for all life on Earth.

But there is one additional fundamental, one more natural law that you must follow to make a successful shift from "Me" to "We." This law is the key to your ability to abide by all of the others. It is the **Law of Free Will.** This natural law of sustainability states that even though your perceptions and behaviors are strongly influenced by your upbringing, today's dominant cultural worldview, and the physical, political, and economic infrastructure they produced, you have the capacity to change your thinking and practices at any time.

Many of us deny this possibility. We are so afraid of opening our eyes to the myths and falsehoods that control our lives that we fight hard to maintain the status quo even when it harms other people, organisms, and ourselves. We are blind to our capacity to think and act consciously and constructively on our own.

Humans, however, are capable of self-awareness and independent thought. You have a natural ability to reveal, examine, and alter the core assumptions and beliefs that shape your life. This means that, at any time, you can choose to abandon views that do not serve you well, keep those that do, and adopt new ways of seeing and responding to the world that produce substantially better outcomes. **The fifth and final commitment you and the organizations you are involved with must make to realize the shift from "Me" to "We" that is essential to resolving today's many crises, is to choose your own destiny.**

I started this book by describing how our experiences and the prevailing cultural narratives shape our beliefs, and our beliefs shape our actions. Our actions, in turn, create results. If we want to change the results we are getting, we need to change our actions. If we want to act in new ways, we must change our beliefs. This can be difficult because humans naturally exhibit what psychologists call "confirmation bias." This means we constantly seek out and pay attention to information that is consistent with and reaffirms our present way of seeing the world, and ignore or discount views that do not. But, if you are mindful of this tendency, you will be free to change your thinking any time you want. This is empowering knowledge – and one of the few facts you can count on to be true 100% of the time.

The belief that has the most influence on our thinking and activities is that we each exist as separate, independent organisms. The primary source of many of the crises our planet is experiencing is the direct result of our egoistic "Me" state of consciousness where we believe ourselves to exist separately from everything else. When you see the world through the lens of separation and extreme individualism, every challenge you face in life will be interpreted by your mind as a threat. Your fight-or-flight instincts will take over, which reinforce your sense of separateness. This is why so many of us feel isolated. Our minds look for evidence, and interpret every experience, to prove that we are separate and alone.

Human thoughts, however, are never-ending. Thinking merely happens. It starts and stops on its own, whether you want it to or not. When you believe your thoughts without questioning your interpretation of them, when you believe that the notions of separation and extreme individualism that emerge in your mind are synonymous with reality, then frustration and discontent emerge. You might try to quench these feelings with more consumption of resources or by striving for more money, power, or prestige. But when the initial emotional high of these ventures ends, the same old feelings arise again, leaving you in a state of continual discontent. Understanding this is the first step in adopting a new way of seeing and responding to the world.

The starting point for the shift from "Me" to "We" is thus to acknowledge that our thoughts are not reality. Our tendency to break the world into separate pieces is merely an attempt by our minds to gain greater understanding and control over things. The next time your mind tries to trick you into thinking that you are separate from everyone and everything else, or that you do not need to be concerned about cause and effect, the moral implications of your activities, or your trustee responsibilities, don't become attached to it. Instead, just observe it and marvel at your mind's ability to play games. As you develop your capacity to watch yourself thinking and grasping onto notions that are illusions, you will become more mindful of the ways in which you are wholly linked to everything else.

This awareness will not destroy your sense of self. On the contrary, it will enhance your personal identity by helping you become more integrated. Researchers have found that the brain actually physically changes in response to experience. Through a process called neuroplasticity, different experiences activate neural firings that lead to the production of proteins that enable new connections to be made between neurons in the brain. Thus, where and how we focus our attention concentrates our cognitive faculties on different behaviors. When we change the focus of our attention, we change our brains. When we change our brains our habits change. By choosing to focus our minds on different things, we thus have the capacity to alter our thinking and behavior. This means that the more mindful you become of your role in the planet's ecological and social systems, the more self-aware you will become, and the greater your capacity will be to focus on the broader "We."[107]

Choose your own destiny

All social change begins at the individual level. This means that the only place to start the shift from "Me" to "We" is with yourself. Our first reaction, of course, is to claim that others must change. We think that if only big corporations, Wall Street, government, right-wingers, left-wingers, or whoever would change, solutions could be found to today's challenges. But this is merely another trick our minds play – a projection, intended to avoid having to look inward. Reality is that we must start with ourselves.

The 19th-century U.S. politician William Jennings Bryant once said, "Destiny is not a matter of chance, but of choice. Not something to wish for, but to attain." Your destiny, and the destiny of the organizations you are involved with, and society at large, will be determined by the choices you make now and in the immediate future.

On a personal level you can choose to continue with business-as-usual. You can, for example, choose to continue to consume, and waste, large amounts of energy derived from fossil fuels. You can choose to continue to buy numerous non-essential products, such as electronic equipment that require massive amounts of energy to produce and operate. You can choose not to ask what those products are made from and what the consequences of their production, use, and end-of-life practices are for people, the biosphere, and the climate. You can also choose to allow corporate interests, politicians and others that are controlled by powerful "Me First and Only" beliefs to advance policies that promote their self-interest while destroying life on Earth. And you can choose to believe that today's huge discrepancies in income and wealth are solely the result of the hard work, efficiency, and intelligence of a select few rather than public policies.

Similarly, your organization can choose to continue with what it is already doing. It can choose to claim that it has no choice but to engage in the same unsustainable practices as its competitors. It can choose to believe that the activities occurring throughout its entire value-chain do little harm to the planet's ecological and social systems, or that the impacts are not its responsibility. It can choose to promote advertising campaigns that provide a veneer of sustainability while in reality allowing business-as-usual to dominate the organization. It can choose to employ marketing strategies that pray on the status insecurities of people to get them to buy products and services they don't need and cannot afford because they feel compelled to keep up with others.

Or you and your organization can make different choices. Be aware that whatever choices you make now will not just affect you. Your choices will shape the options that future generations will have as well. You are choosing the future.

If you choose to make the shift from "Me" to "We" that is essential to resolving today's many crises, you can start by acknowledging the natural laws of sustainability and decide to abide by the commitments described in this book. Likewise, the organizations you are involved with can choose to make the transition from "Me" to "We" and strive to create a culture of accountability for sustainability organized around the five commitments.

Let's explore how to make those choices a reality.

The process of self-change

By understanding the process people go through whenever they make a fundamental change in thinking and behavior, you can gain insight into how you might motivate yourself to embrace the five commitments. Change happens through a series of stages, starting with disinterest and ending with active engagement.

The 'disinterest stage' of change

Prior to the disintegration of his business and family life, Steve Aherns felt no need to change his ways. In the same way, most people start the change process in a state of **disinterest**. This is the "not ready to change" stage of the transition from "Me" to "We." People in a state of disinterest don't give much thought to the possibility that their ways of thinking and acting might be unhelpful or harmful. Any problems that occur as a result of their way of seeing the world are quickly minimized or rationalized away.

There is nothing inherently wrong with being in a state of disinterest. It's where all change begins. Changing our hard-won ways of thinking and acting requires a great deal of energy, so we all want to continue doing what we are already doing. People resist the notion that climate disruption, degradation of the biosphere, and economic inequity are real and serious problems because acknowledging them would threaten their worldview. Troubles arise for people who are disinterested when they stay stuck in this stage even when the drawbacks of their existing approaches are obvious to others or cause significant personal suffering.

There are generally four reasons why people tend to remain firmly stuck in a state of disinterest regarding climate disruption, the biodiversity crisis, and other sustainability issues: reluctance; rebellion; resignation; and rationalization.

Some people are *reluctant* to change due to inertia, fear, or comfort with their current condition. Reluctant individuals make it a point never to learn about climate disruption, economic inequality, or similar issues. Their disinterest is consequently passive. They are not very invested in their current way of thinking or acting.

Rebellious individuals, in contrast, are often very knowledgeable and highly invested in their dysfunctional behaviors. They vehemently oppose any suggestion that their current ways of thinking or behaving might be harmful to others, the natural environment, or themselves. Their rebellion is typically caused by factors such as prolonged adolescence, overcompensation for a lack of self-confidence, or fear of lost opportunities such as profits made from environmentally or socially harmful activities.

People who feel *resigned* to their current condition typically lack motivation. They tend to be overwhelmed by issues such as climate disruption, biodiversity loss, or economic inequity. They also lack confidence in their ability to change their own thinking and behavior. They might have tried to lose weight, give up smoking, or in other ways attempted to make a personal change in the past but failed, felt foolish, and gave up.

Rationalizers are sure they know it all. They might believe they will never be personally affected by climate disruption or other problems of unsustainability, or have the capacity to easily avoid it. When they can't explain away risks, rationalizers almost always project the responsibility for a problem onto other people or onto forces over which they have no control. An example is the claim by many climate deniers that today's climate disruption is merely a natural cycle.

To move beyond a state of disinterest, people must feel a sufficient level of internal emotional or psychological tension, or "dissonance," between their current ways of thinking and acting and how they ideally desire to see and respond to the world. Psychologists know that humans have a strong need for conformity between their internal values and motivations and their external actions.[108] When a gap exists between their current and a desired condition, the emotional energy needed to motivate people to consider the possibility of making a change can emerge.

The 'deliberation stage' of change

When a slight crack in their armor occurs, and people are willing to at least consider the possibility of making a shift, they enter the **deliberation** stage of change. This is the "I might change" stage of the transition from "Me" to "We" where people begin to deliberate about whether or not to alter their thinking and behavior.

During this stage people weigh the pros and cons of making a fundamental shift. Generally, in order to decide to make a change they need to see at least two upsides for every downside. A number of drawbacks might exist, but people are often willing to make a major adjustment in their perspectives if there are at least twice as many benefits.

In addition to issues such as high financial costs and the level of difficulty, one of the most powerful downsides to change is often the reaction of the people involved with an individual's immediate social system. People will decide a change is not worth the effort if their family, close friends, or co-workers will not support or, worse, strongly oppose it. Conversely, people can be motivated to make a change when they decide it will allow them to feel good about themselves because they are living up to their most deeply held moral beliefs.

The 'design stage' of change

If an individual concludes that the pros of making a change far outweigh the cons, and that a shift in thinking and behavior would be beneficial, they enter the **design** stage of change. This is the "I will change" stage of the shift from "Me" to "We" where they establish goals and design a plan to make the change. Making a plan is often an essential step in the change process. A plan keeps you focused on your goals. Sometimes the planning stage of change is rapid, and at other times it can take quite some time. That's because as people design a plan, they are also imagining what they would look and feel like during the change period and afterwards. People make a final decision to change only after they have envisioned themselves in a new condition and decided that the new "them" is beneficial. When they come to this conclusion, they generally tell family, friends, or in other ways make a public commitment to shift their thinking and behavior.

The 'doing stage' of change

After people publicly declare their intention to change, they enter the **doing** stage of change. This is the "I am changing" stage of the transition from "Me" to "We" where people implement the initial plan they designed. The doing stage is both exciting and difficult. As people see themselves changing, their self-confidence grows, their spirits rise, and their energy levels increase. Their selfless behavior fills them with a sense of integrity and honor. Yet change can be difficult because old habits must be abandoned, people often encounter resistance from others, and numerous structural barriers must be overcome. A positive outlook and the willingness to persevere are important.

The 'defending stage' of change

If people implement their initial plan and conclude that it was a positive experience, they often desire to do more. They then enter the **defending** stage of change. This is the "I have changed" stage of the shift from "Me" to "We" where they constantly defend their new thinking and behavior against numerous roadblocks until it becomes routine.

As you read these words, were you able to "stage" yourself? Could you identify where you stand in the transition from "Me" to "We"? If so, you can employ specific change mechanisms to motivate yourself to move to the next stage of change.

Change mechanisms

Moving beyond disinterest

If you classified yourself as in the disinterest stage of the transition from "Me" to "We," one of the most important change mechanisms you can employ is to reframe your perspective. Cognitive reframing is important in each state of change, particularly in the early stages. The process involves recognizing your current way of seeing the world and the behaviors this generates, intentionally questioning unfounded, distorted or dysfunctional beliefs, and then adopting new outlooks that are more helpful.

Four basic change mechanisms contribute to the cognitive reframing process: disturbances; awareness-building; choice expansion; and supportive relationships.

Whether they are climate disruption-induced disasters such as Hurricane Irene that whacked the East Coast of the U.S. in 2011, personal crises such as the type Steve Aherns experienced, or pressure from friends and family, significant disturbances often force us to pull the curtains back and look at the fallacies of our current perspectives. Whether you are disinterested due to reluctance to change, rebellion, resignation, or an ability to rationalize away potential risks, always be ready and willing to use the shock created by a disturbance to ask yourself if your existing way of looking at and responding to the world contributed to, or prepared you for, the crises, and if it will allow you to respond effectively. Using disturbances in this way to open yourself to the possibility of change is especially useful if you are a rebellious or rationalizing disinterested person because it builds "dissonance" between your current state of awareness and real-world conditions.

A disturbance can "unfreeze" your thinking, but the process is reactive. There are a number of proactive steps you can take to move beyond disinterest as well. These change mechanisms can be especially helpful if you are a reluctant or resigned disinterested person because they help to build "dissonance." A helpful change mechanism is awareness-building. Don't confuse this with education. A common misperception is that people become motivated to change their thinking and behavior when they obtain new information. This can be true when the change is simple and does not threaten their deeply held views about the world. But the assumption that an "information deficit" prevents fundamental changes in perception and activities is wrong. Due to the process of "confirmation bias" previously discussed, and the fact that misinformation sticks in our minds even when accurate facts are presented, few people change merely by obtaining more information. Instead, for new information to be helpful in motivating self-change, you must be willing to honestly compare it to your existing beliefs and acknowledge any misperceptions or erroneous conclusions. This is difficult for many people, but when successful it helps to build the "dissonance" needed to promote change.

For example, if you don't know much about climate disruption you can learn about the issue from scientific organizations such as the Intergovernmental Panel on Climate Change (IPCC).[109] You can also seek out stories of how and why people similar to you have altered their thinking and behaviors about the issue. Then ask yourself if your current thought processes and activities might help resolve or add to the climate crisis. Your answer can help you decide if you want to consider a new approach.

One of the reasons some people stay disinterested in dealing with climate disruption or other sustainability issues is a fear that the problems are too big or too complicated to resolve. When you think this way, a helpful solution is to identify a number of small concrete steps you can take. The feeling of being overwhelmed often drops away when you expand the choices that are available for making a change. This process can increase your sense of efficacy, or confidence in your ability to make the change. It also can illuminate some of the benefits of the change.

The thought of making a significant change in thinking and behavior can generate considerable stress. You might stay disinterested in making a shift from "Me" to "We" unless someone you trust is available to confide in and provide encouragement. Humans can do remarkable things when they feel accepted and supported by others. Finding someone to talk with that will support you through the process of change is therefore essential for disinterested people. You might also consider helping someone else. Giving assistance to others often motivates us to change ourselves.

Your use of one or more of these change mechanisms can help you decide if the risks of remaining completely closed to the possibility of making a shift from "Me" to "We" are worth it. If you decide that you are willing to at least consider the possibility of change, you are ready to move to the deliberation stage.

Moving beyond deliberation

When you begin to deliberate about whether or not to make a shift toward sustainable thinking and action your primary task is to determine if the benefits of a new approach outweigh the costs. If, after assessing the situation, you conclude that the pros are equal to or less than the cons, you will likely stay stuck in deliberation or even move back into disinterest. If you decide that the advantages far outweigh the downsides, you will likely move to the design stage of change.

Continued awareness-building, choice expansion, and supportive relationships are important change mechanisms at this stage. So are emotional inspiration, goal-setting, and self-appraisal.

The more information you can gather and the more aware you become of issues such as climate disruption and economic inequity, the greater your ability will be to determine if altering your behavior will prove beneficial to you.

Goal-setting is especially helpful in raising your awareness.[110] Setting a limited number of clear goals can help guide the information-gathering process. For instance, you might choose an initial goal of learning about your home energy use rather than broader topics related to climate disruption. After you set some goals, try to collect credible data that can help you learn about this issue. You might ask your local utility, for example, about how your home energy use compares to other people with similar-size homes in your community. After you have thoroughly investigated your first topic, move on to another one.

Researchers have found that goal-setting is a very powerful motivator of change.[111] That's one of the reasons I have suggested that you make a commitment to understand and abide by the five natural laws described in this book. A commitment is a direct form of goal-setting that can compel significant change.

As you build your awareness, continue also to explore a range of ways in which you might engage in sustainable thinking and action. Investigate a number of incremental steps. The more options you have for manageable step-wise change, the greater the chance that your sense of efficacy and the benefits of the change will grow, and your fears will diminish. Similarly, it will be important to maintain a relationship with someone who will support your desire to examine the potential for making a shift. Keep asking for reactions to your ideas. If you are up to it, ask for candid feedback on whether or not you are seeing the issues clearly, or whether you are being defensive and skewing your evaluation.

To these change mechanisms you should add the opportunity to become emotionally inspired. Often, the way to break through the fear of making a change is to personally see or experience the effects of climate disruption, biodiversity loss, economic inequality, and other problems. You might look for pictures of the parched soils and dead trees caused by the 2011 drought in Texas, or the destruction of homes and property from the tornadoes and hurricanes that occurred that year. Alternatively, you could visit an unemployment center or a homeless shelter, and experience firsthand some of the results of economic inequality. The emotional distress that can occur, and the sense of relief that results from making a decision to do what you can to resolve these problems, can be a potent stimulus for change.[112]

Each of the change mechanisms I just mentioned can be helpful. However, the most important change mechanism if you are in the deliberation stage is self-appraisal.[113] This involves deciding if your current "Me"-focused thinking and activities allow you to be the person you really want to be. To answer this question you must determine if your present way of considering and responding to the world allows you to live up to the aspirations and moral values you hold most dear. This process helps to produce the dissonance needed to move beyond deliberation while also building your self-confidence and clarifying the benefits of making the shift. If you decide that you are not acting in a way that allows you to be the person you want to be, you can choose to do something about it.

After you have spent time engaging in these change mechanisms, make a list of the pros and cons of engaging in sustainable thinking and action. Be as honest and as thorough as you can. Give special attention to the upsides and downsides of change for yourself and for people who are close to you because their reaction might have a powerful affect on your willingness to change. Then decide if the advantages outweigh the disadvantages. If they do, you are ready to move on to the design stage.

If you decide that the downsides are equal or greater than the upsides and you are not ready to move to the next stage, that's OK. Go back through your list and make sure you have sufficiently fleshed out the pros and cons. Then analyze the downsides to determine which might be permanent and which are just temporary. If most of the cons are only temporary (which is often the case with sustainability change efforts) you can then decide if you are willing to put up with some short-term discomfort in order to obtain long-term benefits.

Moving beyond the design stage

If you are ready to move to the next stage of change, it is time to make a plan for how you will make the initial shift from "Me" to "We." The design stage is a very important step in the change process. That is because planning in advance when, where, and how you will complete a self-assigned goal produces greater success. This process is called "implementation intention."[114] Implementation intentions help you move towards your goals and, over time, allow the process to feel automatic. This is especially true for goals that are particularly challenging, which is often the case when you initially decide to make the shift from "Me" to "We" and engage in sustainable thinking and action. Making explicit goals for yourself such as: "I will strive to understand which people and ecological systems my actions might affect," or: "I will act in accordance with the moral obligations to 'do no harm' and 'do good'," is a powerful way of implementing specific changes in your thinking and behavior.

A good initial change plan includes a limited number of clear goals, a small set of actions that will be taken to achieve these goals, and continual monitoring, usually with the help of a trusted confidant.

The power of establishing limited number of concrete goals highlights that making a commitment to change is the most important change mechanism in the design stage.[115] Again, that's why I have framed the focus of this book around the "five transformational commitments" involved with the shift from "Me" to "We." Making a definitive vow to consider and live in accordance with the natural laws of sustainability can establish a positive vision in your mind of how to treat other people, the natural environment, and yourself, now and in the future.

Identifying a limited number of clear steps you can take to achieve your goals is also important because it simplifies the change process. If you can imagine yourself accomplishing the goals, your sense of efficacy as well as the benefits of change will expand. As you experience success, your confidence will grow. Your capacity for self-control will expand as your confidence increases because automatic mental processes will be triggered that don't require much energy or thought.

Continued self-appraisal and supportive relationships are also essential elements in the design stage. Reflecting on who you want to be and how you want to treat others keeps your commitment level high. Maintaining close contact with someone who supports your desire to think and act sustainably can provide a ready-made monitoring mechanism. This person can observe your progress, provide honest feedback, especially in regard to your defense mechanisms, and offer reinforcement that can keeps your spirits high.

The planning stage of change need not be long. But it needs to be thorough enough to give you a good sense of the initial steps you will take to make the shift from "Me" to "We" and engage in sustainable thinking. The design stage should also help you prepare for things that don't go as planned, as always happens when making any type of significant change.

After you believe your plan to be sufficiently robust, it is time to decide if you are willing to make a firm commitment to change. If so, tell someone important what you are going to do, and set a date for when you will do it. The more people you tell about your commitment, and the more specific you are about when you will begin to act, the more likely you are to follow through.[116] Your public commitment to change moves you into the doing stage.

Moving beyond the doing stage

The shift from "Me" to "We" is hard work. It will take effort. As we have discussed, systems always push back hardest when a change is imminent. As soon as you begin to actively engage in sustainable thinking and action, you are sure to encounter barriers. If you are like other people, you will want to avoid circumstances that produce discomfort. In order to avoid the procrastination or delays that might occur as you run into obstacles, you need to be prepared with specific strategies.

One of the most important needs in the doing stage is to keep a positive attitude. Your efforts to overcome hurdles are more likely to succeed if you see them as temporary challenges rather than permanent obstructions.

Obtaining positive reinforcement when you think and act from the perspective of "We," and replacing factors that cause you to backslide into "Me First and Only" thinking and behavior are also important change mechanisms. For example, you might need to avoid people who are unsupportive, and find people to hang out with who are engaged in similar efforts.

Positive reinforcement lifts your spirits and expands your belief in the benefits of making the shift. When someone recognizes your commitment to change as well as your accomplishments, your energy levels will rise and your commitment to making the shift from "Me" to "We" will be solidified. Maintaining supportive relationships is important in this stage because these individuals can monitor your progress and provide you with crucial positive reinforcement.

You can also establish your own reward system. You can, for instance, buy yourself a special treat whenever you find yourself considering all of the consequences of a possible action, or thinking about the moral implications.

Making an effort to identify and eliminate factors that trigger your old unsustainable thought patterns is also important. Trying to make the shift from "Me" to "We" without replacing factors that elicit unsustainable thinking and behavior with those that encourage sustainable action is certain to produce frustration. This should be one of your top priorities. Psychologists call this "counter-conditioning."

Moving to the defending stage

After making the effort to shift from "Me" to "We" for about six months or so, the initial plan you designed should be implemented. Your primary goal now becomes figuring out how to make your pledge to abide by the five commitments stick, grow, and become as automatic as your former "Me"-focused perspective. This is never easy because you will likely continue to run into a raft of physical, structural, and social obstacles. Remember that making "We"-based thinking and action routine takes time. The defending stage of the shift to a sustainable perspective may take years. It is therefore the most difficult stage. Yet it can also be the most enjoyable part of the change process because you are becoming the person you truly want to be.

The change mechanisms of reinforcement and substitution that were used in the doing stage are helpful when defending your shift from "Me" to "We." As in the previous stage of change, you should continue to regularly monitor your progress and explicitly acknowledge your accomplishments. Recognizing and rewarding yourself on a continual basis for success helps to build efficacy and the benefits that will help counter the difficult times.

In addition, the way in which you design the personal, work, and leisure aspects of your life will go a long way in determining your capacity to maintain a "We" perspective over the long term.

Seek out ways to redesign your house, garden, food purchasing, product consumption, and transportation patterns in order to dramatically reduce greenhouse gases, protect the natural environment, and support social and economic equity. You might need to find new friends to hang out with. If your job forces you to think and act from a "Me" perspective, discuss the problem with co-workers and senior executives, and work with them to change the structure of the organization. If that doesn't work, you may need to relocate to a new place of work.

Throughout the entire change process keep your chin up. You will undoubtedly fall back into "Me"-based thinking and action every now and then. Don't berate yourself, or think that you can't make the shift to a "We" perspective. Humans mostly learn by making mistakes. Setbacks do not mean failure. Quite the opposite is true. Failure provides the best opportunities to learn and improve. Keep focused on learning rather than expecting never-ending success. This will help you take a setback in your stride and continue onward. If you embrace this attitude, you will succeed.

Self-awareness: the most powerful change mechanism

Throughout the entire process of self-change the more aware you become of your thinking, emotions, and behaviors – and their consequences for other people, the natural environment, and yourself – the greater your chance of moving through the stages of change all the way to the defending stage of the shift from "Me" to "We." Self-awareness is the most powerful of all change mechanisms because it enhances self-regulation. Almost every spiritual tradition and sage throughout history has said that a direct link exists between self-awareness and self-control. The ancient wisdom has been affirmed by numerous psychological studies that show that greater self-awareness enhances self-regulation, which produces numerous personal benefits.[117] Becoming increasingly mindful of the assumptions and concepts that shape your perceptions, beliefs, and behaviors is far and away the most potent enabler of self-change.

The process of self-change can enhance integration

In Chapter 1 of this book I said that healthy systems are integrated. All of the elements and processes that make up a system function together in relative harmony. Your willingness to honestly examine and challenge your current thinking and actions in order to make the shift from "Me" to "We" can help you become internally integrated. Over time, sustainable thinking and action will become routine. When this occurs, you will no longer be tempted to fall back into "Me"-based unsustainable patterns.

The importance of knowing the stages of self-change

The approach to self-change just described is a modification of the trans-theoretical model of change (TTM).[118] The TTM model resulted from extensive research that distilled 24 major approaches to cognitive and behavioral change into a single framework.[119] I translated TTM into the sustainability-focused "5-D" approach to change that was described in one of my previous books, *The Power of Sustainable Thinking*.[120] TTM researchers, and others, determined that although there were many differences among the various approaches to change, they all coalesce around a key point: people go through a series of stages whenever they make a significant change in thinking and behavior. Each stage of change is fairly predictable, each can be diagnosed, and successful movement through each stage to the next requires that people complete a specific set of internal cognitive activities.

As you engage in the shift from "Me" to "We" make sure you know which stage of change you are in. Then, use the change mechanisms described here to motivate yourself to move to the next stage. There are numerous techniques available for implementing a change mechanism. For example, there are many ways to build your awareness of climate disruption in the early stages of change, and to provide rewards and reinforcement for successful actions in the later stages. The key point is to use the right change mechanisms at every stage.

If you misdiagnose your stage of change, or use change mechanisms that are better designed for other stages, you run the risk of delaying or undermining your efforts. This is a common problem with people striving to engage in sustainable thinking and action. Either they are not aware of their stage of change, or they use inappropriate change mechanisms. For example, some people want to quickly do things when they move out of disinterest into the deliberation stage of change, even though they are not actually ready to act. In some cases this is driven by the unconscious desire to fail, which allows the individual to claim that it is not possible to make the shift from "Me" to "We." Or, when people are in the doing stage and are already engaging in sustainable thinking and actions, they focus on obtaining more information about how bad climate disruption might be when they should spend their time finding ways to overcome obstacles.

The three keys to change

Let me repeat the three closely linked keys to self-change that TTM and other researchers have identified. First, in order for someone to want to make an important change they must feel a sufficient level of tension or dissonance between their current thinking and behavior and different deeply held moral values or personal aspirations. Think about it. If everything in your life seems fine, why would you consider making a change? No tension, no change.

Second, to make a significant change people need to feel a sufficient level of "efficacy" or confidence in their ability to do what is necessary to reduce the dissonance. People must see how the change will happen before they believe it can happen. On a personal level, an individual must believe they have the know-how or skills to make the shift from "Me" to "We," or can get access to the needed resources. In the public arena, efficacy means that people must believe the policies they are being asked to support will actually solve the problem. If people don't believe they can solve the problem and reduce the dissonance, they are likely to stay stuck in disinterest or deliberation.

Third, people must believe that the advantages of making a change far outweigh the disadvantages. They might be willing to learn new skills and take a chance on failure, if they believe the benefits of making the shift seem large enough. But if the perceived pros don't substantially outweigh the cons, they are not likely to make the effort. In the early stages of change it is therefore essential to emphasize the benefits. The downsides will become apparent on their own as people run into numerous obstacles during the doing and defending stages.

All three keys to change – sufficient levels of dissonance, efficacy, and benefits – must be present for people to abide by the five commitments and make the shift from 'Me" to "We." When you engage in the process, keep evaluating how you feel about those factors. If you do not feel sufficiently strong in any area, spend time beefing it up.

Motivating others to change

The same process can be used to motivate other people to make the shift from "Me" to "We," whether they be family members, friends, or people you work with.

To help other people, teams, or organizations make the transition from "Me" to "We" and engage in sustainable thinking and action, start by diagnosing their stage of change. This can be accomplished by asking some simple questions. For example, ask people whether they have engaged in sustainable activities in the past 30 days or whether they have at least considered the possibility of engaging in such activities in the past month or so. If they answer yes to the first question, they are already acting and are likely to be in the doing or maybe even the defending stage of change. If they say that they are considering the possibility of becoming engaged in the next month or so, then they are likely to be in the design stage. If they say they have never considered such actions, then they are in the disinterest stage of change.

After you get a sense of what stage of change they are in, you must use the change mechanisms that are most appropriate for that stage. For example, if the individual you spoke with is in the disinterest stage, strike up a conversation about recent floods, windstorms, or heat waves and ask what they think of these and other extreme weather events unfolding around the planet. You might then offer to provide them with information about climate change, without trying to change their minds about the issue.

The next time an extreme weather event occurs such as a horrific hurricane or massive flood, ask the individual if he or she had a chance to read the climate information and if they think there is a chance that the issues might be related. You could also share photos of horrific damage that occurred. This might create the intellectual or emotional "dissonance" needed to motivate change.

If they respond by saying something like: "I'm not convinced climate change is real but I'm willing to consider the possibility," you know they have moved to the deliberation stage of change. When this occurs, use the change mechanisms that are most helpful in the deliberation stage to motivate the individual to move to the next stage.

Note that compared to people in other stages, people in the disinterest stage of change can be the most resistant to the notion of adopting new views and behaviors. This is especially true for rebellious individuals and those who use rationalization to remain disinterested. Even though these people can be very vocal resistors, they are a minority. Don't get discouraged if you don't see much progress. If, after some effort, you don't see forward movement don't expend all of your energy on disinterested individuals. The vast majority of people reside in the deliberation and design stages of change on climate disruption and other sustainability issues. Focusing your time and energy on these individuals will often reap greater rewards. As more people move to the later stages of change, disinterested people become more isolated which will make some of them more open to the possibility of changing their thinking and behavior.

Remember also that you must build a sufficient sense of dissonance, efficacy, and benefits to motivate people to change. Each of these keys to the successful shift from "Me" to "We" is important, but different people will respond to different factors. One individual, for example, might be most influenced by their sense of the pros and cons of the change, while another might be more heavily influenced by the efficacy they feel in their ability to make the shift. This underscores the importance of constantly focusing on all three keys to change.

Organizations can make the shift from 'Me' to 'We'

Public, private, and non-profit organizations of any type and size can make the shift from "Me" to "We" by acknowledging the natural laws of sustainability and abiding by the five commitments. Your goal should be to create a culture of accountability for sustainable thinking and action in your organization.

Think of the process of organizational change as a pyramid.[121] At the top of the pyramid are the results of your organization's practices, products, and policies. They include all financial, social, and environmental results.

Below the results are the actions that occur within the organizations that produce the results. By actions I mean the behavior of employees, the way goods and services are made and delivered, the quantity and type of energy and raw materials purchased and used, transportation patterns, how employees are treated, how community members are dealt with, and many other practices, programs, and policies.

Below the actions are the beliefs people hold within the organization that lead them to act as they do. This might include the conviction that the organization's sole purpose is to make a profit, that meeting the minimum requirements of environmental laws is sufficient, that using the cheapest materials and least expensive sources of labor is always a priority, or many other such views.

At the base of the pyramid are the experiences people have had outside of, and within, the organization that create and reinforce their beliefs. Employees might see the CEO driving a gas-guzzling SUV, for example, and deduce that despite the organization's professed commitment to the environment, it is not a real priority. Or they might live through a number of "efficiency improvements" that lead to large lay-offs leading them to conclude that the only thing that matters is keeping profits and shareholder value high. Every experience people have creates or reinforces specific beliefs.

The "second-order" cultural change required for the transition from "Me" to "We" in your organization necessitates that changes be made in each of the four core areas of the pyramid: experiences; beliefs; actions; and results.

Most sustainability efforts focus on what people do – on actions – which is the top of the pyramid of change. Focusing on actions alone, however, produces limited results. People often scurry around developing action plans, measures, and vision statements, or installing solar panels and the like. When they meet the goals laid out in the plans they stop and wait for someone to tell them what to do next. A culture of activity is created rather than a culture of accountability for sustainable thinking and actions.

Here is an important point to remember – your organization's results are in many ways determined by its culture. Either you create a culture focused on "We" or your "Me"-oriented norms and values will block all meaningful sustainability efforts.

By a culture of "accountability for sustainability" I mean that rather than people being held accountable only when things go wrong, such as a pollution spill, a common set of accepted beliefs, behaviors, and actions becomes established, along with systems and structures to support them, that lead people to think and act in ways that enhance the social and ecological systems the organization is embedded within – the broader "We."

Each organization should spend as much time establishing this type of accountability as they do in planning and implementing actions such as improving energy efficiency and installing solar panels. This requires a focus on each level of the pyramid of change.

Start by helping people take responsibility for the organization's existing results by engaging them in a facilitated process to identify all of the results, both good and bad. Then have them identify all of the actions that produce those results. Next, move on and ask people to unearth the beliefs that dominate the organization that lead to these actions. Finally, ask them to list the past and current experiences that lead them to hold the beliefs they do.

Although sometimes difficult, this process allows people to take responsibility for the organization's existing outcomes and the culture that produces them. After people overcome the distress of realizing what they are doing and why, they often become energized because they realize that if they created the existing results they have the power to produce different outcomes.

Once this initial step is completed, focus on the "second-order" changes necessary to make the shift from "Me" to "We." Start by asking people to identify the results the organization must achieve to make the shift from "Me"- to "We"-oriented sustainable thinking and action. For example, what would the organization's social and ecological footprints look like, what products and services would it sell, and how would they help restore the planet's deteriorating systems rather than adding to the problems?

Then identify the actions needed to achieve those results. For instance, what materials and substances will be needed to provide those services, how will they be produced, distributed, and marketed, and how should work flows be organized?

After the actions have been identified, work backwards once again to identify the beliefs people must hold to implement those actions. For instance, employees might need to believe they are authorized to make decisions that protect and restore the environment, even if those choices reduce profits or market share. Or they might need to believe that the organization will always put the health and well-being of employees and the wider community ahead of shareholder profits.

Finally, ask people to describe the experiences they need to have within the organization to crystallize and reinforce the new beliefs. They might say, for instance, that to become convinced that the organization is truly committed to sustainability, they need to see the senior executives "walk the talk." Flying around in private jets would undermine their confidence. They might also need to see the organization make a conscious decision to stop producing and selling products made of plastics derived from fossil fuels or those that require extensive use of energy to operate, are embedded with toxic substances, or cannot be completely recycled.

After this process is complete, compare the two lists of results, actions, beliefs, and experiences and hold a thorough discussion at all levels of the organization to identify the benefits of making the "second-order" shift from "Me" to "We." Many organizations struggle to see the benefits of sustainability because they function within a market system that does not reward responsible behavior. Consequently, they don't see how this type of change can come about without going bankrupt, which benefits no one.

This view is almost always based on misperceptions. People believe that the obstacles to true sustainability are permanent and insurmountable. They fail to understand that most of the impediments are short-term. Numerous strategies can then be identified to overcome them. Once the transition is complete, numerous benefits begin to accrue.

Make a list of all of the obstacles people in the organization see standing in the way of the shift from "Me" to "We," as well as all of the benefits the organization would obtain if it made the change. When the list is complete, go through and identify which barriers are short-term and can be overcome with concerted effort, and which ones are permanent. Upon close inspection, invariably 99% of the obstacles turn out to be short-term and numerous strategies can be identified to overcome them. On the other hand, the benefits are almost always permanent. This is an extremely enlightening process. It shows that if the organization can endure through the transition period it will end up substantially better off.

When this discussion is nearing an end, action plans, complete with timelines, responsibilities, etc. should be developed and implemented to guide the transition to sustainable thinking and action.

Throughout the entire process of organizational rethinking and revamping, remember the three keys to change: people and organizations must feel sufficient levels of dissonance, efficacy, and sense of benefits. Also, remember that individuals and groups move through a series of stages when they make a deep-seated change in thinking or behavior, and different change mechanisms will be needed in each stage.

The five commitments enable you to choose your own destiny

Whether your focus is self-change or you want to motivate other people or entire organizations make the shift from "Me" to "We," it is important to be clear about what you want. When you hold thoughts front and center in your mind aimed at positive, constructive purposes, you can control your own destiny. Your determination, which is based on your convictions and intentions, will shape your future. Making a commitment to achieve a specific goal or attain a specific outcome is the most powerful driver available to make the shift from "Me" to "We."

Resolutions, whether made at New Year or at other times, are rarely kept. That's because when a commitment does not serve a higher purpose in our lives, there is little motivation to follow through. In addition, if the intention is little more than a wish, it will have little impact.

If you focus your mind on commitments that are personally meaningful and deeply sincere, and you continually repeat behaviors to achieve them, there is little you cannot accomplish. The power of resolve combined with constant repetition concentrates your mind. In other words, a pledge or commitment binds you to achieve meaningful goals. If you vow to abide by the five commitments with sincerity and persistence, it means you are obligating yourself to focusing on "We," rather than on "Me" alone. You are the agent of change over whom you have the most control. If you decide to do so, you can make the shift from "Me" to "We" and choose your own destiny.

7
Conclusion
It is up to you

So many people I talk with, from CEOs, to government leaders and members of the public, sense that the systems they have long relied on are collapsing and that we have entered a period of volatile change. They intuitively know their old ways of thinking and acting will be of little use in navigating this complex era and are looking for fresh approaches.

Even as they seek a different approach, many people see the five commitments (see Box 1) required for the shift from "Me" to "We" as being difficult to achieve or even beyond the capacity of us mere mortals. But the millions of individuals and organizations engaged in the process suggest the transition has already begun. The primary need is to accelerate and broaden the change to include many more people and organizations. As this occurs, our forces will be mobilized and tremendous innovation will be unleashed leading to the adoption of thousands of new practices, technologies, and policies in a difficult but winnable decade or so. If we fail to do what is necessary to make the shift from "Me" to "We," humanity will face a millennium of adversity.

Box 1: **The Five Commitments Required for the Shift from 'Me' to 'We'**

Natural Law of Sustainability	Commitment
Law of Interdependence	**See the ecological, social, and economic systems of which you are part**
Law of Cause and Effect	**Be accountable for all of the consequences of your actions** on those systems
Law of Moral Justice	When responding to those consequences **abide by society's most deeply held universal principles of morality and justice**
Law of Trusteeship	Respond to those consequences as well by **acknowledging your trustee obligations and taking responsibility for the continuation of all life on the planet**
Law of Free Will	Break free from the false beliefs that control your life and your organization and **choose your own destiny**

Although some people question our capacity to make the transition, the reality is that humans are skilled at changing. In fact, you have changed your personal thinking and behavior many times. Your outlook shifted when you took your first steps as a child. You changed your perspective when you went to school for the first time. You adopted new views when you entered adolescence. You altered your thinking when you got your first job, and probably adjusted it with each subsequent position. Your assumptions and beliefs undoubtedly changed yet again if you lived with someone or married. And they will certainly change many more times as you age. Even though you might believe otherwise, you are good at change.

As a species, humans have also continuously adjusted their perspectives and behaviors. As we discussed in Chapter 1, as human consciousness expanded, we made the shift from hunter–gatherers to farmers and then to members of industrial societies. We made the shift from walking as our primary source of travel to using animals, then to building ships and wagons, then trains, automobiles, airplanes, and spacecraft. Many parts of the world shifted from using vegetation and dung as their primary energy sources, to windmills and waterwheels, to burning coal, oil, and gas, then nuclear, to today's solar photovoltaics, wind turbines, and other high-tech renewable energy sources. Human communications have changed from primitive sign paintings, to simple writing, to the telegraph, to telephones, and then to digital communications first through phone lines and now through cables and satellites. Politically, much of the Western world has transitioned from small clans to warlords, to kings and queens, to representative governments, to the complex multinational agreements, protocols, and laws that we see today.

We must never forget these and the many other profound changes in thinking and behaviors that humans have made throughout time. Looking back, each of the shifts must have seemed impossible before they happened. People living in each era couldn't possibly imagine a different way of thinking or acting. But conditions changed and forward-thinking people realized they needed to shift their perspectives as well. After the changes took place, they seemed totally logical and natural.

Similarly, the shift from "Me" to "We" and the mainstreaming of sustainable thinking and behavior is not a pipe dream. The worldview of separation and extreme individualism that has led so many people to believe that continual self-focused material acquisition is natural and the only way life can be has lasted for almost 300 years. Many people now realize it is no longer a useful way to think, and so it is breaking down. After more people engage, the shift from "Me" to "We" will seem totally natural.

As you engage in this transition, don't get on your high horse and try to force rapid change on others – at least not directly. Instead, inspire them to move one stage at a time through the stages of change. Remember that what others see and hear, and how they respond to the world, is completely shaped by their beliefs, which are based on the same misperceptions about how the world works that you were taught.

Have compassion for others

Deep compassion is needed when you reflect on how often people and organizations ignore the five natural laws of sustainability, and cause so much suffering in the process. Don't condemn them. Our fellow travelers are not inherently bad. At different times of our lives, most of us suffer from a lack of motivation to honestly examine the truth and accuracy of the concepts and assumptions that control our lives, and the cultural narratives that reinforce them.

Have compassion for yourself

Most importantly, don't judge yourself harshly for past mistakes. Understand that it was the erroneous beliefs in the separation of all things, adopted in part from instinctual urges and continually reinforced by the people and institutions you trusted, that led you to believe that an exclusive focus on "Me" was natural and indeed the only way life could be.

Also, remember that the transition from "Me" to "We" will not eliminate all of our troubles. Some people will always struggle to consistently abide by the five natural laws of sustainability. Making a commitment to acknowledge and abide by these laws will, however, allow you and others to make wise choices about the changes in lifestyles, technologies, and policies needed to withstand the turmoil ahead and help society resolve its pressing problems. It will also help expand awareness of the vast opportunities that exist to enhance social and ecological well-being. Most importantly, it will help you achieve personal fulfillment by aligning the way you think and act with the infinite intelligence that pervades all things.

Change happens one person at a time. This means there is only one way to alter the trajectory of the troubling conditions the world faces today, and that is for you to make the shift from "Me" to "We." You must see for yourself the truths inherent in the natural laws of sustainability and the power of the five commitments. If you focus on the broader "We" that makes all life possible, and think and act sustainably, you will find great peace and happiness and become a role model that others will follow.

Endnotes

Introduction

1. D. Keltner, *Born to Be Good: The Science of a Meaningful Life* (New York: W.W. Norton & Co., 2009): 71-73.
2. Intergovernmental Panel on Climate Change, *IPCC Fourth Assessment Report: Climate Change 2007* (www.ipcc.ch/publications_and_dara/publications_and_data_reports.shtml).
3. This quote is said to appear on the so-called Emerald Tablet that legend says was found in the caved tomb of Hermes.
4. Proverbs 23:7. This quote is an abridged version used by James Allen in his wonderful book *As a Man Thinketh* (Cambridge, UK: Cambridge University Press, 1902).
5. *Unappropriated Millions* (www.hinduwebsite.com/selfdevt/texts/secret/tsoa16.asp, accessed 15 November 2010).
6. Thich Chon-Thien, *The Concept of Personality Revealed through the Pancanikaya* (Institute of Buddhist Studies, Saigon, Vietnam, www.budsas.org/ebud/personality/person-22.htm).
7. Quote attributed to the chair of the board of the DuPont Corporation.
8. Unfortunately, CFC substitutes, hydrochlorofluorocarbons (HCFCs), are now thought to contribute to global warming.
9. The terms "first-order change" and "second-order change" were adapted from Gregory Bateson who described them in *Mind and Nature: A Necessary Unity* (New York: Hampton Press, 1979).

10 P. Hawken, *Blessed Unrest: How the Largest Movement in the World Came Into Being and Why No-one Saw it Coming* (New York: Viking Press, 2007).

Chapter 1

11 This is a true story based on the experience of a friend. Personal details have been changed to protect identities.
12 F.L. Gross, *Introducing Erik Erikson: An Invitation to His Thinking* (Lanham, MD: University Press of America, 1987).
13 For a wonderful description of societies that failed to adjust their thinking, see R. Edgerton, *Sick Societies: Challenging the Myth of Primitive Harmony* (New York: The Free Press, 1992).
14 A. Sabloff, *Reordering the Natural World: Humans and Animals in the City* (Toronto: University of Toronto Press, 2001).
15 J.B. Bury, *The Invasion of Europe by the Barbarians* (New York: W.W. Norton & Co., 2000) and G. Halsall, *Barbarian Migrations and the Roman West* (Cambridge, UK: Cambridge University Press, 2007).
16 C. Merchant, *The Death of Nature: Women, Ecology and the Scientific Revolution* (San Francisco: Harper, 1980).
17 M. Bloch, *Feudal Society* (trans. L.A. Manyon; Chicago: University of Chicago Press, 1961).
18 C. Merchant, *The Death of Nature: Women, Ecology and the Scientific Revolution* (San Francisco: Harper, 1980).
19 *Ibid.*
20 D.B. MacPhearson, *The Political Theory of Possessive Individualism: Hobbes to Locke* (Oxford and London: Clarendon Press).
21 *Ibid.*
22 *Ibid.*
23 First published in 1776, *An Inquiry into the Nature and Causes of the Wealth of Nations* was collated into five versions by a team led by Edwin Cannan.
24 This framework is a modification of those that were collectively termed the "dominant social paradigm" by D. Pirages and P. Ehrlich (*Ark II: Social Response to Environmental Imperatives* [New York: Viking Press, 1974]).
25 E.A. Donahue, *The New Freedom: Individualism and Collectivism in the Social Lives of Americans* (New Brunswick, NJ: Transaction Publishers, 1990).

Chapter 2

26 D. Meadows, *Thinking in Systems: A Primer* (White River Junction, VT: Chelsea Green Publishing, 2008): 12.
27 K. Wilber, *No Boundary: Eastern and Western Approaches to Personal Growth* (Boston, MA: Shambhala Books): 69.
28 *Ibid.*
29 European Geophysical Union (www.egu.eu, 2001).
30 For more information on how inequalities in income and wealth lead to health and social problems that affect rich and poor alike, see R. Wilkinson and K. Pickett, *The Spirit Level: Why Greater Equality Makes Societies Stronger* (New York: Bloomsbury Press, 2010).
31 M. Matousek, *Ethical Wisdom: What Makes Us Good* (New York: Random House, 2011): 153.
32 *Ibid.*
33 R. Baumeister and J. Tierney, *Willpower: Rediscovering the Greatest Human Strength* (New York: Penguin Books, 2011): 114.
34 D. Siegel, *Mindsight: The New Science of Personal Transformation* (New York: Bantam Books, 2010): 40-41.
35 R. Wilkinson and K. Pickett, *The Spirit Level: Why Greater Equality Makes Societies Stronger* (New York: Bloomsbury Press, 2001).
36 See, for example: B. Hagerty and R.A. Williams, 'The effects of sense of belonging, social support, conflict, and loneliness on depression', *Nursing Research* 48.4 (July/August 1999): 215-19; and B. Hagerty, R. Williams, J. Coyne, and M Early, 'Sense of belonging and indicators of social and psychological functioning', *Archives of Psychiatric Nursing* 10.4 (August 1996): 235-44.
37 J.C. Barefoot, K.E. Maynard, J.C. Beckham, B.H. Brummett, K. Hooker, and I.C. Seigler, 'Trust, health, and longevity', *Journal of Behavioral Medicine* 21.6 (1998): 517-26; D. Subramanian, D. Kim, and I. Kawachi, 'Social trust and self-related health in U.S. communities: a multilevel analysis', *Journal of Urban Health* 79.4 (2002, Supplemental I): 21-34.
38 See, for example, D. Kim, 'Guidelines for drawing causal loop diagrams', *The Systems Thinker* 3.1 (thesystemsthinker.com/tstgdlines.html); and *MindTools* (www.mindtools.com/pages/article/newTMC_04.htm).

Chapter 3

39 Intergovernmental Panel on Climate Change, *IPCC Fourth Assessment Report: Climate Change 2007* (www.ipcc.ch/publications_and_data/publications_and_data_reports.shtml).

40 T. Loster, *Flood Trends and Global Change* (Geoscience Research Group, Munich Reinsurance Company, www.iiasa.ac.at/Research/RMS/june99/papers/loster.pdf, June 1999).

41 G. Meehl, C. Tebaldi, G. Walton, D. Easterling, and L. McDaniel, 'Relative increase of record high maximum temperatures compared to record low minimum temperatures', *U.S. Geophysical Research Letters* (www.agu.org/journals/gl/gl0923/2009GL040736, 2009).

42 As described in *Climate Progress* (climateprogress.org/2010/11/26/another-extreme-drought-hits-the-amazon-raising-climate-change-concerns, November 2010).

43 L.A. Wagner, *Materials in the Economy: Materials Flow, Scarcity and the Environment* (U.S. Geological Survey, Circular 1221, 2002).

44 Global Footprint Network, *World Footprint 2011* (www.footprintnetwork.org/en/index.php/GFN/page/world_footprint).

45 D. Siegel, *Mindsight: The New Science of Personal Transformation* (New York: Bantam Books, 2010): 187-89.

46 U.S. Centers for Medicare & Medicaid Services (www.cms.gov/NationalHealthExpendData).

47 European Monitoring Centre for Drugs and Drug Addiction (www.emcdda.europa.eu/data).

48 U.S. Surgeon General, *Denver Post* (www.denverpost.com/nationworld/ci_1681, 9 December 2010).

49 See, for example, the ASQ Quality Tools description of Fishbone diagrams at asq.org/learn-about-quality/cause-analysis-tools/overview/fishbone.html.

Chapter 4

50 This exercise is a slight variation of the "veil of ignorance" described by John Rawls in *A Theory of Justice* (Cambridge, MA: Belknap Press, 1971).

51 M. Matousek, *Ethical Wisdom: What Makes Us Good?* (New York: Random House, 2011): 109.

52 T. Rosenbaum, *The Myth of Moral Justice: Why Our Legal System Fails to Do What's Right* (New York: HarperCollins Publishers, 2004): 4-5.
53 For more information see, for example, E.O. Wilson, *On Human Nature* (Boston, MA: The President and Fellows of Harvard College, 1978): 25-42.
54 These principles are described by Kent M. Keith as the "Universal Moral Code" (www.universalmoralcode.com/code.html, 2003).
55 *Ibid.*
56 *Ibid.*
57 World Health Organization, *Climate and Health* (www.who.int/mediacentre/factsheets/fs266/en/index.html, 2009).
58 Climate Vulnerability Forum and DARA, *Climate Vulnerability Monitor 2010* (daraint.org/climate-vulnerability-monitor/climate-vulnerability-monitor-2010/download-the-report, 2010).
59 *The Human Impact Report: Climate Disruption – The Anatomy of a Silent Crisis* (Geneva: Global Humanitarian Forum, 2009).
60 Briefing of the Director of the American Public Health Association, the President of the American Medical Association, and the Deputy Director of the EPA Pediatric Environmental Health Specialty Unit (www.apha.org/about/news/briefing0224.htm, 25 February 2011).
61 Centers for Disease Control and Prevention (www.cdc.gov/climatechange/effects/waterborne.htm, November 2010).
62 Climate Vulnerability Forum and DARA, *Climate Vulnerability Monitor* 2010 (daraint.org/climate-vulnerability-monitor/climate-vulnerability-monitor-2010/download-the-report).
63 M. Parry, N. Arnell, P. Berry, D. Dodman, S. Fankhauser, C. Hope, S. Kovats, R. Nicholls, D. Satterthwaite, R. Tiffin, and T. Wheeler, *Assessing the Costs of Adapting to Climate Change: A Review of UNFCCC and Other Recent Estimates* (Imperial College London, Grantham Institute for Climate Change, pubs.iied.org/pdfs/11501IIED.pdf, August 2009).
64 Economics for Equity and the Environment (E3) (www.e3network.org/social_cost_carbon.html, 2011).
65 UN Convention on Biological Diversity, *Third Global Biodiversity Outlook* (gbo3.cbd.int).
66 K.M. Brander, 'Global fish production and climate change', *Proceedings of the National Academy of Sciences* 104: 50 (www.pnas.org/content/104/50/19709.long, 6 December 2007).

67 The Universal Declaration of Human Rights was adopted by the UN General Assembly in December 1948 (www.un.org/en/documents/udhr).
68 M. Sandel, *Justice: What's the Right Thing To Do?* (New York: Farrar, Straus & Giroux, 2009): 104.
69 R. Baumeister and J Tierney, *Willpower: Rediscovering the Greatest Human Strength* (New York: Penguin Press, 2011): 113.
70 M. Matousek, *Ethical Wisdom: What Makes Us Good?* (New York: Random House, 2001): 61.
71 *Ibid*: 156.
72 E.O. Wilson, *On Human Nature* (Cambridge, MA: Harvard University Press, 1978): 99-120.
73 J. Fox, J. Levin, and K. Quinet, *The Will to Kill: Making Sense of Senseless Murder* (Boston, MA: Allyn & Bacon, 2007).
74 *Ibid*.
75 UN Framework Convention on Climate Change is an international treaty developed in 1992 (unfccc.int/essential_background/items/6031.php).
76 Lawrence Livermore National Laboratory (https://flowcharts.llnl.gov/energy.html, 2008).
77 McKinsey & Company, *Reducing U.S. Greenhouse Gas Emissions: How Much and At What Cost?* (www.mckinsey.com/en/Client_Service/Sustainability/Latest_thinking/Costcurves.aspx, 2007).
78 Directorate General for Energy and Transport, *2020 Vision: Saving Our Energy* (Brussels: European Commission, www.energy.eu/publications/2007_eeap_en.pdf, 2007).
79 J. Dernbach and D. Brown, *The Ethical Responsibility to Reduce Energy Consumption* (Wilmington, DE and Harrisburg, PA: Widener Law School Legal Studies Research Paper Series No. 09-18, 2010).
80 UN Department of Economic and Social Affairs, Population Division, *World Population to 2300* (New York: United Nations, www.un.org/esa/population/publications/longrange2/WorldPop2300final.pdf, 2004).
81 McKinsey & Company, *Reducing U.S. Greenhouse Gas Emissions: How Much and At What Cost?* (www.mckinsey.com/en/Client_Service/Sustainability/Latest_thinking/Costcurves.aspx, 2007).
82 For more information see www.recovery.gov/About/Pages/The_Act.aspx.

83 See, for example, the U.S. Endangered Species Act 1973 (www.epa.gov/lawsregs/laws/esa.html).
84 R. Wilkinson and K. Pickett, *The Spirit Level: Why Greater Equality Makes Societies Stronger* (New York: Bloomsbury Press, 2010): 235-36.
85 *Ibid.*
86 H. Wallick, *Falling Behind: How Rising Inequality Harms the Middle Class* (New York: Bloomsbury Press, 2007): 221-22.
87 R. Wilkinson and K. Pickett, *The Spirit Level: Why Greater Equality Makes Societies Stronger* (New York: Bloomsbury Press, 2010): 250.
88 T. Rosenbaum, *The Myth of Moral Justice: Why Our Legal System Fails to Do What's Right* (New York: HarperCollins, 2004): 218-40.
89 *Ibid.*
90 R. Wilkinson and K. Pickett, *The Spirit Level: Why Greater Equality Makes Societies Stronger* (New York: Bloomsbury Press, 2010).
91 T. Kasser, *The High Price of Materialism* (Cambridge, MA: The MIT Press, 2002).
92 *Ibid.*
93 Walker Information (www.walkerinfo.com/knowledge-center/default.asp?s=3, 2001).

Chapter 5

94 This picture was obtained from the NASA Visible Earth website (visibleearth.nasa.gov/view.php?id=57723).
95 This term was first coined in 2000 by Paul Crutzen and Eugene Stoermer in Newsletter 41 of the International Geosphere-Biosphere Program.
96 D. Siegel, *Mindsight: The New Science of Personal Transformation* (New York: Bantam Books, 2010): 75.
97 See, for example, the 'General Duties of a Trustee' in the *California Probate Code*, Sections 16000-16042.
98 For more information see, for example, *Public Assets, Private Property, Reclaiming the American Commons in an Age of Market Enclosure*, David Bollier and the New America Foundation, Washington DC, 2001.
99 W. Domhoff, *Who Rules America? Wealth, Income, and Power* (Sociology Department, University of California at Santa Cruz, www2.ucsc.edu/whorulesamerica/power/wealth.html, 2011).

100 National Equality Panel, *An Anatomy of Economic Inequality in the UK* (eprints.lse.ac.uk/28344/1/CASEreport60.pdf, January 2010).
101 *Ibid.*
102 Credit Suisse, *Global Wealth Report* (www.credit-suisse.com/news/en/media_release.jsp?ns=41610, 2010).
103 R. Wilkinson and K. Pickett, *The Spirit Level: Why Greater Equality Makes Societies Stronger* (New York: Bloomsbury Press, 2010).
104 T. Kasser, *The High Price of Materialism* (Cambridge, MA: The MIT Press, 2002).
105 For more information, see W. McDonough and M. Braungart, *Cradle-to-Cradle: Remaking the Way We Make Things* (Boston, MA: North Point Press, 2002).
106 This material is adapted from B. Walker and D. Salt, *Resilience Thinking: Sustaining Ecosystems and People in a Changing World* (Washington, DC: Island Press, 2006).

Chapter 6

107 D. Siegel, *Mindsight: The New Science of Personal Transformation* (New York: Bantam Books, 2010): 84-86.
108 R. Bénabou and J. Tirole, *Incentives and Prosocial Behavior* (Cambridge, MA: National Bureau of Economic Research Working Paper Series, 2005).
109 www.ipcc.ch.
110 J. Prochaska, J. Norcross, and C. DiClemente, *Changing for Good: A Revolutionary Six-Stage Program for Overcoming Bad Habits and Moving Your Life Positively Forward* (New York: Avon Books, 1994).
111 *Ibid.*
112 *Ibid.*
113 *Ibid.*
114 P.M. Gollwitzer and V. Brandstatter, 'Implementation intentions and effective goal pursuit', *Journal of Personality and Social Psychology* 73 (1997): 186-99.
115 J. Prochaska, J. Norcross and C. DiClemente, *Changing for Good: A Revolutionary Six-stage Program for Overcoming Bad Habits and Moving Your Life Positively Forward* (New York: Avon Books, 1994).
116 *Ibid.*

117 R. Baumeister and J. Tierney, *Willpower: Rediscovering the Greatest Human Strength* (New York: Penguin Press, 2011).
118 *Ibid.*
119 *Ibid.*
120 R. Doppelt, *The Power of Sustainable Thinking: How to Create a Positive Future for the Climate, the Planet, Your Organization and Your Life* (London: Earthscan, 2008).
121 For more information about the process of organizational change, see my previous book, *Leading Change toward Sustainability: A Change Management Guide for Business, Government and Civil Society* (Sheffield, UK: Greenleaf Publishing, 2003, 2010).

Index

5-D approach to change   135
   see also Defending stage; Deliberation stage; Design stage; Disinterest stage; Doing stage; Self-change
Accountability
   organizations   112, 120, 140, 141–2
   see also Cause and effect
Acidification of oceans   47–8, 67, 69
Addiction   54, 71
Age of Reason   17
Aherns, Steve   9–11, 22, 121, 125
Alienation   21, 29
All-terrain vehicles (ATVs)   77–8
American Recovery and Reinvestment Act 2009   80
Anthropocene era   93
Anxiety   37, 71, 89
Apartheid   62
Apollo 17   92–3
Arthur Anderson   113
Asthma   66
Atmospheric space   76, 96
Awareness-building   125, 126, 128

Bacteria   25, 31, 50
Bible, The   4
Biosphere   29, 50, 55, 60, 63, 99, 111, 120
   cause and effect and   46–9
   climate system and   30, 31
   degradation   47, 70, 72–3, 81, 121
   "do no harm" principle and   65, 67
   extinction of species   47–8, 59, 67, 81, 85, 86, 114
   human suffering and   67, 81
   meaning   30
   moral justice and   70, 72, 75, 79, 80–1, 89
   photosynthesis   25, 31
   prioritizing   80–1
Biotic communities   30, 31
"Blue Marble"   92–3, 94
Brain size   36–7
Bryant, William Jennings   119
Buddha   4
Businesses
   see Organizations

Calvin, John   18
Cancer   37, 55
Capuchin monkeys   63
Carbon dioxide   30, 79, 82
   deforestation and   45
   extinction of species and   47–8
   ocean acidification and   47–8, 67
   see also Greenhouse gases
Cause and effect, Law of   40–57, 147
   biosphere and   46–9
   climate and   44–6
   family well-being and   54–5
   focus on daily events   42, 43
   greenhouse gases and   45–6, 48–50
   mistaken thinking about   42–3
   optimizing of parts of system   42, 43–4
   organizations and   53–4, 55, 56
   personal well-being and   54–5
   quick fixes   43, 53

Index

social systems and   51–2
symptoms/causes confusion   42, 43, 49
technological capacity and   48–9
time delays   42–3
see also Accountability
Change
  first-order change   6
  organizations   140–4
  second-order change   6, 12, 22, 39, 56, 60, 112, 141, 142, 143
  self-change
    see Self-change
Chimpanzees   63
China   79
Chlorofluorocarbons (CFCs)   5
Choice   6, 7, 71
  choosing your own destiny   119–20, 144–5
  moral choice   84, 89, 90, 91
  organizations and   91, 143
Choice expansion   125, 127, 128
Church   16, 17
  see also Religion
Cigarette smoking   54–5
Climate change/disruption   3, 105, 126, 138, 139
  deaths due to   66
  deforestation and   44, 45, 49, 65–6
  diversity and redundancy   106–7
  drought   3, 46, 59, 73, 78, 106, 107, 129
  duty of prudence and   106–8
  economic consequences   66–7
  floods   46, 59, 66, 78, 106, 107, 138
  greenhouse gases and   45–6, 49, 65–6, 69
  heat waves   3, 46, 59, 78, 106, 138
  human health and   66, 81
  Kyoto Protocol   79
  management for disturbance and change   107–8
  moral justice and   65–6, 69, 76, 80–1, 83, 85
  preparation/adaptation for   106–8
  promoting modularity and   108
  sea-level rise   3, 46, 59, 66, 73, 78, 106
  storms   3, 46, 73, 106, 138
  temperatures
    see Global temperatures
  UN Convention   76
  windstorms   106, 138
Climate deniers   122
Climate system   28, 30–2
  biosphere and   30, 31
  cause and effect and   44–6

Closed-loop systems   104
Cognitive reframing   125–6
Communist regimes   84
Compassion   149–50
Confirmation bias   117, 126
Conflict resolution   73–5
Cooperation   6, 13, 14, 20, 22, 50, 60, 61, 94
Copenhagen climate summit 2009   83
Copernicus   5
Corporate social responsibility (CSR)   112
Counter-conditioning   133
Cradle-to-cradle production systems   104
Cultural development
  see Human cultural development

Dark Ages   16
Defending stage   124–5, 138
  moving to   133–4
  see also Self-change
Deforestation   46, 48, 104–5
  carbon dioxide and   45
  climate change/disruption and   44, 45, 49, 65–6
Deliberation stage   123, 136, 139
  emotional inspiration   129
  goal-setting   128
  moving beyond   127–30
  self-appraisal   129
  see also Self-change
Denmark
  environmental protection   101
  standard of living   100–1
  violence and   74
Depression   37, 71, 89
Descartes, René   17, 18
Design stage   123–4, 138, 139
  goal-setting   123–4, 130–1
  moving beyond   130–2
  see also Self-change
Destiny, choosing your own   115–45, 147
  see also Change; Self-change
Dinosaurs   47
Disclose, duty to   109–10
  see also Trusteeship
Diseases   37, 55, 59, 66
Disinterest stage   121–3, 136
  awareness-building   125, 126
  cognitive reframing   125–6
  dissonance   122–3, 126
  disturbances   125–6
  moving beyond   125–7, 138–9
  rationalization   122, 125, 139
  rebellion   122, 125, 139

reluctance 122, 125
resignation 122, 125
supportive relationships 125
see also Self-change
Dissonance
self-change and 122–3, 126, 129, 137, 139, 144
Diversity and redundancy 106–7
Divorce 68
"Do good" principle 64, 94, 130
see also Trusteeship
"Do no harm" principle 64–5, 88–9, 94, 130
biosphere and 65, 67
cutting consumption 75
duties under 68–9
economic self-interest 79
failure to follow 65–8
human rights and 69
protecting the vulnerable 81
reducing income inequality 85
social systems and 67–8
see also Moral justice
Doing stage 124, 136
moving beyond 132–3
positive reinforcement 132, 133
see also Self-change
Downcycling 104
Drought 3, 46, 59, 73, 78, 106, 107, 129

Ecological debt 75
Ecological footprint 109, 112, 142
Ecological systems
see Ecosystems
Economic growth 21, 67, 70, 76, 80, 83–4, 109
abandoning idea of continuous economic growth 102–3, 104
income inequality and 83
Economic inequality
reducing 83–5, 88
Economic systems 21, 26, 108
economic growth and 76
equality and 84, 103
meaning 33
Economy, the 51–2
climate change and 66–7
closed-loop systems 104
cutting consumption 75–9
moral justice and 87–9
regulation 51

Ecosystems 27, 28, 29, 31, 32, 46–7, 59, 104
degradation 22, 38, 47, 48, 70, 72, 81, 82, 93, 96, 100, 105, 111, 121
forest ecosystems 27, 31
optimizing of parts of 43–4
Einstein, Albert 4, 35
Emotional inspiration 129
Energy consumption 49
cutting 75–9, 87–8
energy value-chains 78
wasted energy 77
Enlightenment, the 17
Enron 113
Entrepreneurship 88
Erikson, Erik 12, 14
Ethnic identity 68
European Commission 77
European Geological Union 32
European Union
emissions 79
wasted energy 77
see also United Kingdom
Extinction of species 47–8, 59, 67, 81, 85, 86, 114

Feudalism 16–17, 35, 52
Financial crash 2007/2008 51–2, 108
First-order change 6
Fishbone diagrams 56
Floods 15, 18
climate change/disruption 46, 59, 66, 78, 106, 107, 138
Foreign aid 83, 101
Forest ecosystems 27, 31
Forests 36, 96
biotic communities 31
deforestation 44, 45, 46, 48, 49, 65–6, 104–5
oxygen generation 25, 27
trees 28, 31, 35, 36
Fossil fuels 49, 70, 76–7, 78, 113, 119
Free will, Law of 116–45, 147
choosing your own destiny 119–20, 144–5
self-change
see Self-change

Galileo 5
Global temperatures 29, 30
climate change/disruption 3, 30, 45–6, 81, 106
greenhouse gases and 73

Index 163

moral justice and 73, 81–2
rise in 3, 30, 45–6, 67, 73, 81, 106
surface temperatures 3, 30, 31–2, 45
Goal-setting 123–4, 128, 130–1
Golden Rule 59, 65, 94
Government responsibilities 98–100, 109–10, 113
Greenhouse gases 30, 65, 73, 80, 93, 101, 103, 104
  atmospheric space 76, 96
  cause and effect and 45–6, 48–50
  climate change and 45–6, 49, 65–6, 69
  costs of reductions 80
  cutting 78, 80, 82, 106, 134
  deforestation and 45
  global temperatures and 73
  right to emit 76
  see also Carbon dioxide

Heat waves 3, 46, 59, 78, 106, 138
Hermes 4
Hinduism 4
Hobbes, Thomas 18
Human cultural development 14–17, 21, 22–3, 148
Human psychosocial development 12–14, 20, 22
Human rights 5, 63, 69
Hurricane Irene 125

Impartiality, duty of 95, 100–1
Income inequality 34, 37, 52, 84–5, 97, 100, 103, 120
  economic growth and 83
  the market and 84
  see also Wealth inequality
Individualism 2, 20, 65
  extreme 3, 20, 21, 41, 61–3, 70, 93–4, 117, 118
  moral justice and 61–3
Industrial Revolution 19–20, 30, 35, 45
Integration 26–7, 28, 38, 70, 94
  self-change and 118, 135
Interdependence, Law of 25–39, 147
  see also Systems
Intergovernmental Panel on Climate Change (IPCC) 126

Japan 100–1

Kyoto Protocol 79

Lawrence Livermore National Laboratory 77
Living trust
  see Trusteeship
Locke, John 18
Loneliness 21, 29, 37
Loyalty, duty of 95–101
  awareness/acceptance of responsibilities 98–100
  delegation 95–6
  equitable distribution of compensation 97–8
  fair treatment of all beneficiaries 100–1
  government responsibilities 98–100
  impartiality 95, 100–1
  no appropriation of assets for private gain 96–7
  see also Trusteeship
Lung cancer 55
Luther, Martin 18

McKinsey & Company report 77, 79
Market, the 19, 21, 51, 108, 113, 143
  government oversight 99
  income and 84
Material consumption 48, 89–90
  cutting 75–9, 87–8
Mental health problems 66
  see also Anxiety; Depression
Middle Ages 16–17
Modularity 108
Monitor, duty to 109–10
  see also Trusteeship
Monkeys 63
Montreal Protocol 5
Moral justice, Law of 60–91, 147
  economic benefits 87–9
  economic self-interest and 79–80
  global temperatures and 73, 81–2
  individual rights and 61–3
  material and energy consumption 75–9
  morality and justice 60–3
  non-judgmentalism 62
  organizations and 90, 91
  peaceful conflict-resolution 73–5
  personal benefits 89–90
  personal morality 86–7, 91
  prioritizing climate/biosphere 80–1
  protecting the vulnerable 81–2
  reducing economic inequality 83–5
  religion 64
  rescuing the innocent 81–2
  restorative justice 85–6

sources of morality 63–4
"us-versus-them" stereotyping 71–3
see also "Do no harm" principle
Mortgage-selling 52
Mothers Against Drunk Driving 85

Neuroplasticity 118–19
Newton, Isaac 18
  Third Law of Motion 40, 42
Norway
  environmental protection 101
  foreign aid 83
  standard of living 100–1

Ocean acidification 47–8, 67, 69
Organizations
  accountability 112, 120, 140, 141–2
  cause and effect and 53–4, 55, 56
  change 140–4
  choices 91, 143
  choosing own destiny 119–20
  corporate social responsibility (CSR) 112
  diversity and redundancy 106–7
  moral justice and 90, 91
  as social systems 110–11
  sustainable thinking and action 140, 141, 142, 144
  trustee role of business 110–12
Over-connectedness 108
Oxygen 24–5, 27, 31
Ozone layer 5

Pacifism 74–5
Petroleum 49
Phosphate 31
Photosynthesis 25, 31
Population
  increase 48, 49, 73, 78
  reduction programs 76
Precautionary principle 69, 105
Production systems
  redesign 103–4
Protestant ethic 18–19
Prudence, duty of 101–9
  continuous economic growth and 102–3
  education in sustainable thinking and acting 108–9
  investment 101–2
  precautionary principle 105
  preparation/adaptation for climate disruption 106–8

prohibition of speculation 102, 105
redesign of production systems 103–4
sustainable use of resources 104–5
see also Trusteeship
Psychosocial development 12–14, 20, 22

Quick fixes 43, 53

Rationalization 122, 125, 139
Rebellion 122, 125, 139
Reductionism 19
Religion 4, 5
  morality and 63, 64
  see also Church
Reluctance 122, 125
Resignation 122, 125
Resilience/resiliency 27, 70, 106–8
Restitution 85, 86
Restorative justice 85–6
Rio Earth Summit 1992 105

Sea-level rise 3, 46, 59, 66, 73, 78, 106
Second-hand smoking 55
Second order change 6, 12, 22, 39, 112, 141, 142, 143
  moral justice 60
Self
  as rational planner 18
  sense of 12–14
Self-appraisal 129, 131
Self-awareness 117, 134–5
Self-change
  5-D approach 135
  change mechanisms 125–35
  cognitive reframing 125–6
  dissonance and 122–3, 126, 129, 137, 139, 144
  efficacy and benefits 128, 131, 133, 137, 139, 144
  identifying stages 135–6
  integration and 118, 135
  motiving others to change 138–9
  process of 121–5
  self-awareness and 117, 134–5
  stages
    see Defending stage; Deliberation stage; Design stage; Disinterest stage; Doing stage
  tension 137
  three keys to change 137–8, 139, 144
  trans-theoretical model (TTM) 135–6, 137

Self-confidence 8, 12, 122, 124, 129
Self-control 60, 65, 68, 70–1, 131, 134–5
Self-focused worldview 20–3
Self-interest 2–3, 18, 19, 50, 52
Selflessness 2–3, 20, 22
Separation 2–3, 20, 21, 35–6, 38, 41, 117–18
Skin 28
Slavery 5, 62
Smith, Adam 19
Smoking 54–5
  second-hand 55
Social footprint 109, 112, 142
Social systems 26, 27, 28, 29, 32–5, 42, 59
  businesses and 110–11
  cause and effect and 51–2
  "do no harm" principle and 67–8
  economy and 33
  management for disturbance and change 107–8
  optimizing of parts of 43–4
  trust 51
South Africa
  apartheid 62
  Truth and Reconciliation Commission 85
Soviet Union 84
Species extinction 47–8, 59, 67, 81, 85, 86, 114
Sport utility vehicles (SUVs) 77, 140
Stimulus Bill 80
Storms 3, 46, 73
  windstorms 106, 138
Substance abuse 54–5
Supportive relationships 125, 128, 131, 132
Surface temperatures
  see Global temperatures
Sustainable thinking and action 6–7, 8, 71, 87, 135, 138, 148–9
  choosing to engage in 127, 128, 129, 130, 131, 132, 136
  duty to become educated in 108–9
  in organizations 140, 141, 142, 144
  trusteeship and 108–9, 112, 116
Sweden
  environmental protection 101
  foreign aid 83
  standard of living 100–1
  violence and 74
Systems 25–39, 41
  biosphere
    see Biosphere

  climate 28, 30–2, 44–6
  dysfunctional 26–7
  ecological
    see Ecosystems
  economic
    see Economic systems
  healthy 26
  limits 44, 70
  mapping 38
  meaning 27
  optimizing of parts 43–4
  over-connectedness 108
  social
    see Social systems
Sun and Earth 30–2, 44–6, 65

Technological capacity 48–9, 76
Technological change 76, 77, 82, 104
  zero-carbon technologies 89
Temperatures
  see Global temperatures
Thinking
  sustainable
    see Sustainable thinking and action
Trans-theoretical model (TTM) 135–6, 137
  see also Self-change
Transparency 109
Trees 28, 31, 35, 36
  see also Forests
Trust 51, 72, 89, 127, 149
Trusteeship, Law of 93–114, 116, 147
  duty to demand allegiance to trustee responsibilities 112–14
  duty to disclose 109–10
  duty of loyalty
    see Loyalty
  duty to monitor 109–10
  duty of prudence
    see Prudence
  Earth as living trust 94–114
  role of business 110–12

United Kingdom
  emissions 79
  entrepreneurship 88
  foreign aid 83
  individualism 2, 20, 40
  Industrial Revolution 19
  inequality of wealth 37, 97, 101, 103
  see also European Union
United Nations (UN) 5
  climate summits 79

Framework Convention on Climate
    Change   76
United States
  American Recovery and Reinvestment
      Act 2009   80
  emissions   79
  entrepreneurship   88
  financial crisis   52
  foreign aid   83
  individualism   2, 20, 40
  Industrial Revolution   19
  inequality of wealth   37, 97, 101, 103
  material consumption   49
  population increase   48
Universal Declaration of Human
    Rights   69
"Us-versus-them" stereotyping   71–3

Victims' rights programs   85–6
Violence   37
  conflict resolution   73–4

Walker Information   90
Wallich, Henry   83
Waste
  disposal   93
  energy   77
  redesign of production systems   103–4
Wealth inequality   37, 97–8, 101, 103
  see also Income inequality
Weather systems   28, 31
Whitney, Eli   19
Windstorms   106, 138

Zero-carbon economy   88, 89

For Product Safety Concerns and Information please contact our EU representative GPSR@taylorandfrancis.com
Taylor & Francis Verlag GmbH, Kaufingerstraße 24, 80331 München, Germany

www.ingramcontent.com/pod-product-compliance
Lightning Source LLC
Chambersburg PA
CBHW061349300426
44116CB00011B/2057